THE PURITAN TRADITION IN ENGLISH LIFE

THE PURITAN TRADITION

IN

ENGLISH LIFE

By

JOHN MARLOWE

LONDON

THE CRESSET PRESS

1956

First published in 1956
by the Cresset Press Ltd., 11 Fitzroy Square, London, W.1
Printed in Great Britain by The Camelot Press Ltd.,
London and Southampton

TO JEANNE

'. . . the Lord do so to me, and more also, if aught but death part thee and me.'

(Ruth 1.17.)

Note

THIS book is concerned only with English Puritanism. No attempt is made to deal either with the quite separate Puritan movement in Scotland, or with the powerful Puritan movement in the United States, which was a direct descendant of English Puritanism.

My thanks are due to my daughter Sara for assistance with the Index.

Contents

CHAPTER I

Introduction

THE name Puritan appears in English history during the second half of the sixteenth century. Its appearance coincided with the opening of that period of expansion, lasting from the middle of the sixteenth to the end of the nineteenth century, which transformed England from a small island kingdom into the centre of the greatest Empire the world has ever seen. It is the theme of this book that Puritanism provided a moral atmosphere and a continuing influence which helped to sustain and to renew the energy motivating this expansion. It is the purpose of this book to illustrate this theme by an account of the origins, the ideals and the continuing influence of Puritanism.

One of the characteristic features of medieval society was its lack of competitiveness. The pattern of existence, as exemplified in feudal obligations, guild rules, and religious observances, consisted in the performance of certain duties within a defined and accepted sphere of responsibility. Medieval virtues consisted in the cultivation of one's own garden rather than in the breaking of virgin soil; the qualities required to maintain society were those of conservation and appreciation rather than those of innovation and criticism.

The rhythm of a nation's life can be seen in terms of synthesis, expansion, consolidation and decay. In England, after successive harrowings of the land by the Saxons, the Danes and the Normans, synthesis was achieved within the spiritual framework of the Roman Church and within the material framework of the feudal system. The phase of consolidation produced the glories of Gothic art and the social conventions idealized in those highly coloured pictures of Merrie England conjured up by Roman Catholic propagandists and sentimental medievalists of our own day. But these things bore within themselves the seeds of their own decay. Individually the impact of new ideas and new discoveries gave thinking men new horizons of thought and active men new spheres of activity. Socially the despotism of the early Tudors completed the disintegration which the baronial wars had begun.

But this harrowing was the prelude to a new sowing. It was now England's turn to be caught in that upsurge of energy which from time to time seems to overtake certain nations for the achievement of some mysterious end in the cosmic scheme of things. The English people entered on a phase of expansion and power under the driving force of qualities other than those which had sustained and embellished the life of medieval England.

Hard work and capital accumulation are necessary to sustain an age of material expansion. England's progress to material greatness was essentially founded on hard work and capital accumulation. Puritanism was the moral atmosphere which both nourished and was nourished by the practice of hard work and material accumulation. Without this motivating and justifying moral atmosphere, the energy and the self-denial required for this tremendous national effort of self-assertion would soon have become dissipated in the sands of human weakness.

Slowly evolved among those scholars and divines, merchants and craftsmen, yeomen and gentlemen, who for intellectual or for material reasons began in growing numbers and in growing force to challenge and to change the institutions of medieval England, Puritanism emerged in Elizabethan times as the articulate expression of a new age, in which competition tended to replace contract, in which free enquiry was esteemed more than inherited tradition, and in which the place to which a man was going was more important than the place from which he had come.

During the years in which Puritans were a specific and recognizable group in the community—years which roughly covered the second half of the sixteenth and the first half of the seventeenth centuries, they gradually came to form the militant wing of that opposition to the exercise of the Royal Prerogative which finally brought Charles I to the scaffold. This opposition was motivated by two objects, one negative and the other positive. The negative object was the establishment and extension of freedom from State control in economic and religious affairs. The positive object was the establishment of effective Parliamentary control of the Crown by making the Crown financially dependent on supplies voted by Parliament. The attainment of these objects involved trying to prevent the Crown either from promulgating laws or from raising money by the exercise of the Royal Prerogative.

To some extent all this was merely a continuance of that endemic squabble between Crown and Parliament over money which had been going on in England since the beginning of the thirteenth century. But with this difference. Under the Tudors and Stuarts the various administrative machines built by such men as Thomas Cromwell, Strafford and Laud attempted a far more comprehensive control, needed much more money, demanded a far more rigid obedience, and exacted far more savage penalties than had ever been envisaged by a Plantagenet monarch. And, on the other side, Tudor and Stuart Parliaments were far more independent, far less inhibited, and far more ambitious than any of their predecessors had been. Moreover the House of Commons had behind it an increasingly wealthy, increasingly well-informed, increasingly obstinate and increasingly vocal body of opinion in the urban merchants and country gentry who elected the Commons and from whom its membership was drawn.

Elizabeth and her counsellors, by judicious and voluntary restrictions on the use of the Prerogative, and by timely concessions to the demands of free enterprise, succeeded on the whole in avoiding any serious Parliamentary interference with the business of government. But under the Stuarts the claim of the Commons to limit the exercise of the Royal Prerogative developed into a life and death struggle with the Crown for the sovereignty of the State. By the end of this struggle, the Commons, victorious over the Crown, itself became dominated and finally abolished by its own militant allies.

It is tempting to regard that select, stalwart band of

jack-booted, grim-faced religious fanatics whom we associate with the Cromwellian dictatorship, embittered as they were with persecution, exalted by fighting, and arrogant from success, as being the lunatic fringe of the Puritan movement, and as being unrepresentative of the main body of Puritanism. But it would be a mistake to imagine that Puritanism, in its heyday, was distinguished by sobriety either in its religious convictions, its behaviour, or in its methods of controversy. The Puritans were fanatics, both in opposition and in power. Their fanaticism led them to break with and to overpower the country squires and city magnates who had been their allies in the struggle against the Crown. It was Cromwell's great achievement that he did not allow this Puritan fanaticism to plunge the country into chaos. But he could not prevent this fanaticism from discrediting the Commonwealth in the eyes of the majority of the Commonwealth's citizens. Qualities which had been exaggerated into defects during the process of struggling for power proved incompatible with the continued exercise of power. Puritanism was unable to pass the acid test to which all revolutionary movements are subjected—the test of ability to change its habit of mind from one of effective opposition to one of effective authority. And so, with the Restoration, Puritanism, as a specific and recognizable movement, dissolved and died. But, at almost exactly the point where Puritan power ceased, Puritan influence may be said to have begun. The great upsurge of religious fanaticism and social intolerance, which in so strange a way combined a passion for freedom with a love of discipline, a rejection of tradition with an insistence on authority, which had tamed a Tudor Queen and killed a Stuart King, which had brought Laud and Strafford to the scaffold, and which, in spite of its illiberal intolerance, had laid the foundations of liberty and tolerance in England, did not disappear from history at the Restoration any more than classical Athens disappeared from history after its conquest by Macedon. Like Athens, its posthumous influence was more enduring, more beneficent, and more important than its political history. Puritanism was destroyed as a political power by its excesses; it survived as a social influence through its virtues and, in the centuries to come, left its mark on almost every aspect of English life.

For a hundred years Puritanism had been associated with material success. After the Restoration, the popular reaction from Puritanism, and the operation of the Penal Laws, drove Puritanism down the social and economic scale until Puritans came to consider the special favour of the Almighty as being the consolation for material failure rather than the justification of material success. For the next hundred and fifty years politics became the plaything of rival aristocratic cliques. The victory of Parliament over the Crown was finally accomplished by a gang of cynical, corrupt and profligate politicians who were actuated by no discoverable motive either of principle or of passion. Principle and passion were gradually extruded both from politics and from established religion. All those vital forces which had flared up in England some hundred years before seemed to have been driven underground where, beneath the surface of the polite minuets of eighteenth-century party strife and dynastic warfare, other more important but less publicised activities increased England's monetary wealth and agricultural and industrial productivity as a prelude to the further upsurge of expansive energy which began to make itself manifest during the second half of the eighteenth century.

While the aristocrats were losing our American colonies, hardy and prolific growths of inventive genius, organizing ability and driving force were thrusting their way upwards. The Enclosures —that long and relentless process of eviction and spoliation which since Tudor times had accompanied the steady improvement of English agricultural techniques—had destroyed the independence and eroded the vitality of the yeoman class. The reservoir of human enterprise which was for a hundred and fifty years to pump a continual supply of energy and inventiveness through the stream of English life, was mainly an urban one, made up of manufacturers, small professional men, tradesmen, artisans, and craftsmen of all kinds. Puritanism, in the process of its disintegration into numberless dissenting sects of peculiar people, had merged imperceptibly into the sombre texture of

English middle-class life and, diluted and diffused so as to conform with the Zeitgeist of the eighteenth century, was adopted as a way of life by humble people striving for material success. The discipline of hard work and the capital accumulation required for such material success found their inspiration and their justification in that strange mixture of pride and humility, of self-denial and selfishness, which is part of the paradox of English Puritanism.

And so, behind the inventiveness, the acquisitiveness, the ruthlessness and the tireless energy of industrial England in the nineteenth century we shall find, among other things, the driving force of a form of Christianity which owed more to the Old than to the New Testament, and which was motivated less by the hope of comfort in this world than by the certainty of Salvation in the next. But there was another and gentler side to nineteenth-century Puritanism. The Evangelical Movement, inspiring most of that social conscience and those works of organized charity which mitigated the ruthless competitiveness of the Industrial Revolution, was deeply imbued with Puritanism and represented, as it were, the right wing of the Puritan tradition. The left wing embraced and accompanied the forces of Nonconformity in their material and spiritual progress through nineteenth-century England, and infected the post-Whig Liberal Party with its enthusiasm for the twin virtues of sober living and free enterprise.

When, towards the end of the nineteenth century, the pillars of Christian belief seemed to be buckling beneath the weight of scientific discovery, and the movement of economic forces tended to turn men's ambitions from economic adventure to economic security, Puritanism ceased to be a vital factor in English life. The Labour Party and the Trades Union Movement, although on the fringe of the Puritan tradition, lacked the essential Puritan elements as a result of their predominantly secular outlook, their emphasis on State assistance rather than self-help, and on the redistribution rather than the production of wealth. The main body of Puritanism tended to retire to a last ditch manned principally by the economic advocates of 'the small man' and the religious opponents of sacramentalism.

6

An economic climate of Protection, 'rationalization' and monopoly capitalism was matched by a social climate of agnosticism, increasing sexual licence, and a growing pre-occupation with amusement. This economic and social climate, together with the disintegrating influence of two world wars, combined to erode and to destroy among the generality of Englishmen those standards of behaviour and belief which Puritanism had contributed to English life and by which Puritanism had helped England to prosper and to become great.

Today it seems that Puritanism has no distinctive and vital place in English life. But the story may not yet be over. There may be another harrowing and Puritanism may once more seep upwards through English society to colour another age with its sober hue and to harden another generation of Englishmen with its courage and its determination.

CHAPTER II

The Historical Background of English Puritanism

PURITANISM has been defined by Professor G. M. Trevelyan as 'the religion of all those who wished either to purify the usage of the Established Church from the taint of Papacy, or to worship separately by forms so purified'.

Although Puritanism attracted and developed other than religious strains in the English character, it was, in its origin, essentially a religious movement. It has become fashionable in High Anglican circles to regard the English Reformation merely as a manœuvre motivated by the political ambitions, financial greed, and bodily lusts of King Henry VIII. In fact, Henry VIII aimed to accomplish, and did accomplish, nothing more than the deposition of the Pope from temporal and spiritual dominion over England, and the spoliation of the monastic Orders. The liturgical and doctrinal changes which followed these acts of State were not necessitated by these acts, nor, for the most part, were they desired or demanded by those who had implemented or benefited from these acts. But this political Reformation did precipitate the eruption of a moral, intellectual and spiritual ferment which had been slowly maturing among educated Englishmen since the days of Wyclif and the Lollards over 100 years before. The increasing ignorance, venality and idleness of a majority of the clergy, which resulted in an increasing perfunctoriness in the performance of their duties of preaching, teaching, and the administration of the Sacraments (and, in the case of the monasteries, almsgiving), affronted the hearts and minds of very many people who were completely untainted by any shadow of scepticism about the literal truth of the Christian revelation. These people came to regard the clergy, and to some extent the Church itself, as parodying rather than interpreting the Word of God.

Thus they turned from the Church and clergy to the Bible itself. English Puritanism was nourished in the womb by a study of the Bible, both in the Vulgate and in vernacular translations. In medieval times there was a general belief in the literal inspiration both of the Old and of the New Testaments, and access to the Bible by laymen inevitably meant that the Word of God as contained in the Bible was quoted as an authority overriding the pronouncements of priests, bishops, and popes. It is not surprising that the Church was perennially concerned to deny direct access by laymen to Holy Scripture. In the minds of those heretics who insisted on such direct access, the Bible not only came to supersede the Church as a source of authority, but, in the long run more importantly, study of the Bible came to supersede the Sacraments of the Church as a means of Grace.

Up to the time of the political Reformation, access to the vernacular Bible was limited to comparatively few people. The more generalized access which became possible after the political Reformation caused an impact on the minds of the English people which it is almost impossible to over-estimate. It was an age of ample leisure and few books. It was an age quite untouched either by the scepticism of the scientist or by the rationalizations of the philosopher. The Church was becoming discredited, in so far as it was becoming discredited, not because its miraculous pretensions strained men's credulity, but because its mundane inefficiency failed to satisfy men's imagination. 'The hungry sheep looked up and were not fed.'

The vernacular Bible provided the spiritual food which was lacking to feed the imaginations, the faith and the loyalty of thousands of English people. In many—perhaps in most—minds the attraction of this new revelation of God (for that is what the vernacular Bible must have seemed) was counterbalanced by the pull still exercised by the traditional ways. This attraction and counter-attraction was the basis of the Anglican Establishment which in essence was a compromise between the Catholic and the Protestant, between the Sacramental and the Evangelical, view of Christianity. It was a compromise, not in the sense of its being a mere political convenience, nor in the sense of its being

an arbitrary combination between two incompatibles, but in the
sense of its being a liturgical and doctrinal expression of the religious synthesis achieved by the majority of educated Englishmen.

The Puritans were those who, both inside and outside the
Establishment, rejected almost *in toto* the Sacramental aspect of
Christianity and, in general, those aspects of Christianity which
depended on belief in the Apostolic Succession, in favour of an
interpretation of Christianity based on justification by faith
alone and a belief in the literal inspiration of the Bible. (Belief
in justification by faith implied belief in Salvation as a definite
and attainable state, bearing fruit in works, which were seen
not as a condition of ultimate Salvation but as witnesses to a
state of Salvation already attained. This belief struck at the heart
of any conception of the Church, or of the Sacraments administered by the Church, as being a continuing vehicle of Divine
Grace.)

The Elizabethan Establishment inevitably, in the light of the
spirit of the time, regarding conformity as synonymous with
loyalty, and not wishing to make conformity too difficult, tried
to be sufficiently tolerant in its administration as to enable the
majority of Puritans, both clerics and laymen, to remain within
the Establishment. But there was an element of fanaticism, an
element of revolutionary zeal, at the core of Puritanism, which
made it impossible that it should be entirely contained within
the four corners of an Establishment intended for men and women
who were neither fanatics nor revolutionaries. During the first
half of the seventeenth century this fanaticism and this revolutionary zeal were to leave their indelible mark on England. But,
during the reign of Elizabeth, the fanatics played an insignificant
and, to all appearance, inglorious role.

During Elizabeth's reign the vast majority of Puritans were
'nonconformist' rather than 'separatist' in that, although they felt
unable to conform to the Establishment as it then existed, they
concentrated their efforts on trying to reform the Establishment
from within. The 'separatists', on the other hand, rejected the
whole concept of a national Church in favour of independent
'gathered' congregations of like-minded believers. In the next

century, partly as a result of the logic of Puritan thinking and partly as a result of stricter Anglican discipline, Puritanism was to become almost synonymous with separatism. But in Elizabeth's reign separatism was confirmed to a few sects—such as the Barrowites and the Browneites—who were identified (erroneously) with the Continental Anabaptists, regarded with horror by respectable people, and ruthlessly persecuted. Nonconformity was illegal but regarded as respectable. Separatism was treasonable and regarded as damnable.

Outstanding among the nonconforming Elizabethan Puritans was Dr. Thomas Cartwright, a Fellow of Trinity College Cambridge and Lady Margaret Professor of Divinity. He has been described as 'the first Puritan to take his stand boldly on the Scriptures as the court of appeal for discipline as well as doctrine'. In his writings he maintained that diocesan episcopacy had no basis in Scripture and ought to be abolished. He advocated that Ministers should be elected by congregations. His translation of *Ecclesiasticae Disciplinae Explicatio* by Walter Travers became 'the canonical handbook of presbyterian nonconformity'. For his writings Cartwright was deprived of his professorship in 1570 and of his fellowship in the following year. In 1574 he fled abroad to escape arrest. Meanwhile nonconformist Puritanism had been making its voice heard in Parliament. In 1571 a Bill was introduced into the Commons by Strickland, a Puritan Member, for the reform of the 1560 Prayer Book. The Government objected on the ground of interference with the Royal Prerogative and Strickland was haled before the Privy Council. In 1572 the Queen sent a message to the Speaker to the effect that no Bills on religious subjects should be introduced into Parliament until they had first been considered and approved by the Bishops in Convocation. This marked the end of Puritan activity in Parliament during Elizabeth's reign. During the last two decades of the century Church discipline, exercised through Ecclesiastical Commissions, was greatly intensified by Archbishop Whitgift (who became Archbishop of Canterbury in 1583) to deal with nonconforming Puritans, and many clergy suspected of nonconformity were deprived.

It is stated by Bishop Mathew in *Social Structure in Caroline England* that 'the fiery zeal of the nonconformists reflected the religious approach of the unenfranchised' and that 'an element of social inequity and religious discrimination were required to keep that flame alive'. This may have been true after the Restoration, but in Elizabeth's reign the Puritans included many country gentlemen, officials and even courtiers (including Sir Amyas Paulet, Mary Queen of Scots' last gaoler), as well as a large number of rich London merchants. The Elizabethan Puritans soon became conspicuous by reason of the sombreness of their clothing (in an age when men and women delighted in as bright colours and as rich stuffs as they could afford), by the mannerisms of their speech, and by the unbridled violence of their criticisms of other people's behaviour. The somewhat unattractive Puritan characteristics (a contemporary, Thomas Nashe, wrote of them that 'they speak as though they had been brought up all their days on bread and water, . . . as though they had been eunuchs from their cradles or blind from the time of their conception') which can be seen in the pamphlets of men like Philip Stubbes, their curmudgeonly attitude towards harmless amusements and recreations, derived directly, if not entirely logically, from their religious beliefs, and were not merely, or even mainly, a manifestation of envy against the pleasures of the rich. (It may more reasonably be objected that they were harder on the amusements of the poor than they were on those of the rich.)

One of those aspects of Catholic Christianity which had attracted most criticism from the Reformers was the popular medieval belief that last-minute repentance would completely atone for an evil life. 'Between the stirrup and the ground, I mercy asked, I mercy found.' This belief was encouraged by the system of Indulgences, and by the importance which the Church attached to the Sacrament of Extreme Unction. (That this was not merely a medieval Roman superstition seems to be implied by the words of the Roman Catholic burial service in which sudden death is regarded as a particular evil, and by some curious passages in the works of contemporary English Roman Catholic novelists.) Puritan morality was a reaction of personal responsibility against the medieval man's tacit contract with the Church by which he was relieved of moral obligation in return for spiritual submission. Like all reactions, it was violent and excessive and was, moreover, accentuated in Elizabethan England by reason of the Italianate licentiousness which was beginning to become fashionable and which was even more odious to the Puritans than the conventional moral laxity of the medieval Roman Catholic.

If the Elizabethan Puritans were out of tune with the spirit of the time in the matter of personal morals, they were at one with the majority of their contemporaries in their extreme nationalism. (Extreme nationalism can, and frequently does, co-exist with the apeing of foreign manners.) English Roman Catholics inevitably suffered from papal and jesuitical attempts to incite them to, and to implicate them in, acts of treason. But Puritanism carried with it no implication of foreign intrigue. When Stubbes had his right hand cut off for publishing a scurrilous pamphlet protesting against the Queen's marriage negotiations with Anjou, he raised his hat with his left hand and shouted 'God Save the Queen', amid the shocked and sympathetic murmurs of the case-hardened Elizabethan onlookers. No such gesture would have been conceivable from, and no such respect would have been accorded to, a Roman Catholic rebel. Puritans had everything to lose, as Roman Catholics had everything to gain, from invasion by, or even from defeat at the hands of, a European Power, which, at that time, was synonymous with a Roman Catholic Power.

There does not appear to have developed among the Elizabethan Puritans any specific and recognizable opposition to the exercise of the Royal Prerogative in other than religious matters. The sustained and successful opposition to Monopolies, which was the principal achievement of Elizabeth's last Parliament, was not a specifically Puritan performance. But it was the first round of a fight for the sovereignty of the English State, in which the Puritans were first to combine with and then to absorb the English squirearchy and burgesses as represented in the House of Commons.

By the end of Elizabeth's reign overt Puritan nonconformity had been driven underground and all but crushed by the persecution of Archbishop Whitgift. As a result of this persecution, overt Puritan sentiment was confined to vociferous criticism of, and, in London, where there were strong Puritan influences in the City administration, to active interference with, public amusements and contemporary morals.

Meanwhile, within the Established Church, the minds of administrators and theologians were being exercised by the problem of trying to combine the greatest possible measure of comprehension with the greatest possible measure of uniformity. Liturgical uniformity was imposed by the Prayer Book. A generous measure of doctrinal latitude was permitted by the Thirty-nine Articles. In his *Book of Advertisements* issued in 1566, Archbishop Parker attempted to impose some sort of uniformity in the matter of vestments and church furniture. On the one hand it was difficult to impose uniformity on what was essentially a doctrinal compromise. On the other hand lack of uniformity would insidiously have led to a measure of toleration and to an extent of indiscipline which, at that time, would have reduced the Establishment to a nullity. Essentially the problem before the Establishment was the same then as it still is to-day, with the important exception that, in Elizabethan times, loyalty to the Established Church was regarded as part of a subject's loyalty to the State. Hooker, in his *Laws of Ecclesiastical Polity*, published in 1595, attempted to refute both Puritans and Catholics by producing a philosophical and doctrinal apologia for the Via Media of the Anglican Establishment. On the one hand Hooker argued that 'no one form of Church Government is prescribed as an immutable pattern by the Divine Word', thus justifying the Reformation in general and in particular denying the validity of the doctrine of the Apostolic Succession and, consequently, the divine origin of episcopacy. On the other hand he attacked the Puritan belief in the all-sufficiency of the Scriptures, and maintained that the authoritative interpretation of the Scriptures was the function of the Church.

Anglican practice in Elizabethan times went a very long way

in the direction of satisfying the prejudices of the more moderate of the nonconforming Puritans. This helps to explain the later Puritan reaction towards separatism when the Establishment under Laud reverted to what the Puritans regarded as Romanising tendencies. (Laud's 'Romanising tendencies' can in fact, in so far as vestments, Church furniture, rubrics, etc. are concerned, be regarded as the mean of current Anglican practice.)

At the beginning of the new reign two distinct points of view began to become apparent among the Puritans. One party wished to have their own beliefs and practices given a secure legal sanction. The other party wished to convert the Establishment to its own beliefs and practices. Both these points of view found expression in the Millenary Petition which was presented to James I soon after his accession by several hundred Puritan clergy. On the one hand the Petition asked that clergy should not be required to declare their belief in the absolute truth of the whole Prayer Book, and that they should be allowed some choice in the use of vestments. On the other hand the Petition demanded the disuse of the sign of the Cross in Baptism, the abolition of bowing at the name of Jesus, the abridgement of the Prayer Book service, the simplification of music and chanting, and the non-observance of Saints' Days. In addition there were some at all events theoretically uncontroversial demands such as that for the encouragement of the preaching of sermons, the abolition of ecclesiastical sinecures and the stricter observance of Sundays.

The Petitioners were summoned to meet the King and the Bishops in Conference at Hampton Court. At the Conference, mainly as a result of the intransigence displayed on the one side by Bancroft, Bishop of London, and on the other side by Dr. Reynolds, the chief Puritan spokesman, debate was concentrated on a Puritan proposal to limit the power of the Bishops by making it obligatory on them to consult Synods composed of the lower clergy of the diocese.

This proposal for the limitation of the power of the Bishops was the thin end of a very substantial wedge. The Catholic view of Episcopacy was that it was a divinely appointed means of transmitting the Grace of God, in unbroken succession from the Apostles, by means of the laying on of hands in ordination, and was consequently a necessary condition of the spiritual efficacy of the Church's ministrations. It had a further and politically even more important significance. The episcopal anointing of a King, in the same way as the episcopal ordination of a priest, was held to confer a divine sanction on the King so anointed. This had been a dangerous doctrine both for Bishops and for Kings before the Reformation, but, with the King as the Head of the Established Church, its propagation had obvious advantages for both. Its embracement by the Stuart Kings and Anglican Bishops set the course of political events in England for the next hundred years. For the result of the King claiming episcopal anointment as divine justification for the unfettered use of his Prerogative was to identify the secular grievances of the squires and burgesses with the religious grievances of the Puritans and so to create an alliance against absolutism and to save England from the plagues of tyranny and chaos which were to ravage most of the rest of Europe throughout the seventeenth century.

'No Bishop, no King.' With this epigram King James I unwittingly inaugurated that Revolution which in the course of the century was to send one English King to the scaffold and another into exile, and to substitute once and for all the sovereignty of Parliament for the divine right of kings. Others, very different from the Puritans, were to complete what the Puritans had begun. But before the Puritans disappeared from the political scene they had made history. And as they made history they became absorbed into the broad stream of English life as it rolled majestically on towards dominion and power.

The Hampton Court Conference broke up with the King's threat to the Puritans ringing in the ears of the delegates. 'If this be all your party hath to say, I will make them conform themselves or else will harry them out of the land.' These words, spoken in haste by an angry and conceited pedant, set Puritanism on the road from nonconformity to separatism, since, from that time, Puritans began to despair of the possibility, either of obtaining toleration for their beliefs within the Establishment, or of converting the Establishment to their own beliefs. His words also led to the foundation of the constitutional liberties of England and, after many vicissitudes, to the Declaration of Independence of the United States of America. For among the first of those Puritans who were 'harried out of the land' in pursuance of the King's threat were the Pilgrim Fathers, whose descendants, in the fullness of time, challenged the pretensions of George III with the same resolution and with the same ultimate success as their ancestors had challenged the pretensions of James I.

James' first Parliament, which met in 1604, supported the Millenary Petition and the arguments which had been advanced in support of it by the Puritan clergy who were its signatories. It is interesting to consider how far this support—the first overt sign of alliance between the Puritan clergy and the elected representatives of the country gentry and the burgesses of the towns—was due to a conscious common interest in opposition to royal absolutism, and how far to the influence of Puritan religious ideas among the gentry and burgesses.

In medieval times Parliamentary opposition to the Crown had for the most part come from the Barons in the House of Lords who stirred up the Commons to make difficulties over grants of supplies. The power of the Barons had been largely destroyed by the Wars of the Roses and by the subsequent strong centralized administration of the Tudors. When Parliamentary opposition arose again in the last years of Elizabeth's reign the initiative had passed to the Commons where, with some vicissitudes, it has remained ever since. (For most of the eighteenth century effective power was exercised by the magnates of the House of Lords, but they had to exercise this power through the medium of their nominees in the Commons.) For the hundred years between the Battle of Bosworth and the defeat of the Armada, Parliament had been little more than a rubber stamp for the ratification of the Royal will. The emergence of the Commons, towards the end of the sixteenth century, as an organ of criticism and control, was a sign of the emergence of a new age. Just as in religious affairs the old authority of the Church as a counterbalance to royal absolutism, which had been destroyed by the Reformation, was being superseded by the authority of the individual conscience, so, in secular affairs, the old authority of the barons, exercised mainly through their military power, was being superseded by the emergent authority of the heirs of the feudal system—the landed and monied men of the shires and boroughs. This emergent authority was exercised through their elected representatives in the Commons, through their local influence and, finally, when these means had proved insufficient, through the military power which money and local influence could command.

It was not unnatural that there should be close ties of sympathy between the representatives of the new influences emerging in religious and in secular affairs, and it is difficult to disentangle the various strands of self-interest, common peril, and religious affinity which made up those ties. One common principle united them—a common rejection of the concept of unchanging and unquestioned authority derived from tradition and doctrine and obeyed as a divine ordinance, and a common acceptance of the concept of a developing and debatable authority derived from reason and consent and accepted as a matter of discipline and conscience. As this common principle came to be coherently realized, explicitly stated, and resolutely acted upon, so it became opposed by the coherent realization, explicit statement and resolute implementation of the traditional principle, refurbished, rationalized and brought up to date in the form of the doctrine of the Divine Right of Kings, by James I and Charles I, by Laud and Strafford, and by the other Ministers of the Royal will of the Stuart Kings.

As these opposing concepts of the nature of authority became more explicit, so the possibility of moderation on either side became extinguished. When the conflict of principles had fought itself to a standstill, the Restoration marked the exhaustion of principle and the enthronement of a precarious compromise based on conscienceless, rootless and calculated expediency.

The definition of the Royal position emerged whole and complete from the mouth of James I in his speech to his first Parliament. '. . . it is sedition in subjects to dispute what a King may do in height of his power.' He also told them that they 'derived all matters of privilege from him', and that it sat 'not in its own right but of his grace'. Charles I, standing on the scaffold gazing into eternity, was to express the same unequivocal sentiments. 'A subject and a sovereign are clean different things.' The opposite position took longer to clarify itself and was in fact never so precisely nor so unequivocally clarified. A dogmatic position is always more rapidly arrived at and more clearly expressed than an empirical one.

But the royal position had one great and, in the long run, fatal drawback. It lacked the spiritual sanction which the Roman Catholic Church gave to secular absolutism. It lacked the stability of the deep unseen traditional roots which for so long sustained the continental absolutisms of France and Spain. The hankerings after Roman Catholicism displayed by Charles I and II were almost certainly due to a conscious or sub-conscious realization of this deficiency. Laud's attempt to use the Anglican Church as an instrument of coercion failed because the Anglican Church was itself based on a protest against coercion. Laud's 'Romanizing tendencies' in ceremonial and in matters of church furniture were symptoms of a conscious attempt to reintroduce Roman discipline and were resented as such. It was not the idolatry but what they regarded as the sinister symbolism of Roman practices which aroused Puritan ire. In a superstitious age, Puritan beliefs were just as superstitious as Roman beliefs; it was not Roman superstition that Puritans objected to, but the secular uses served by that superstition.

The Parliamentary position owed its strength to the spiritual sanction provided by Puritanism. The nature of secular authority upheld by Parliament was reinforced by the nature of spiritual authority recognized by the Puritans. Secular policy and religious policy were part of an integrated whole. This remained true of all the various parties into which the Puritan-Parliamentary alliance eventually broke up. They were all basically agreed on the nature of authority both in civil and in religious matters.

The political events leading up to the Civil Wars and the

Puritan Revolution can be roughly divided into three periods:

(*a*) from the Millenary Petition in 1603 to the Three Resolutions in 1629, during which time a series of Parliaments summoned fairly regularly offered passive opposition to the exercise of the Royal Prerogative;

(*b*) from the dissolution of Parliament in 1629 to the calling of the Long Parliament in 1640, during which period the King attempted to govern without Parliament, and

(*c*) from the summoning of the Long Parliament in 1640 to the outbreak of the Civil War in 1642, during which period Parliament, under the leadership of Pym, openly and actively asserted the sovereignty of Parliament against the sovereignty of the King.

Immediately after the Hampton Court Conference, some 300 Puritan clergy were deprived of their benefices, but, apart from that, there was, during the first period, no sustained attempt to curtail the permissible bounds of conformity more straitly than in Elizabethan times. In secular affairs, the accumulation of the grievances which had arisen over the previous twenty-five years was summed up in the Petition of Right (1628), when the Commons successfully petitioned the King against Martial Law, billeting, arbitrary taxation and arbitrary imprisonment, and in the Three Resolutions (1629), when the same House of Commons precipitated the dissolution of Parliament by protesting against 'Popish and Arminian' innovations in religion and against the levying of certain indirect taxes (tonnage and poundage) without consent of Parliament.

At this time it does not appear that Parliamentary opposition to the Royal power evoked very much interest or support among ordinary men and women. Stuart absolutism aimed, not at dragooning the masses, but at subjecting the new breed of monied merchants and rich country gentry to the Royal will. The merchants and gentry, for their part, were interested, not in any abstract conception of liberty and justice, but in freedom for themselves and security for their possessions. It was the religious aspect which was to give the dignity of principle to the defence of material interests and to convert a struggle between rival factions into a popular revolution.

Just as in the twentieth century it is inevitable that any major social controversy is seen primarily in terms of economics, so in the seventeenth century it was inevitable that any such controversy should be seen primarily in terms of religion. To-day a man's religion (if he has any) is apt to be dictated by his politics. In the seventeenth century a man's politics (if he had any) were apt to be dictated by his religion. When at last it came to the arbitrament of battle, men chose their side according to their religious rather than their political beliefs, and Falkland and Hyde found themselves in opposition to Pym and Hampden.

It was the incompetence, as well as the oppressiveness, of Charles' attempts at absolute rule during the 1630's that determined the temper of the Long Parliament in 1640. Instead of crushing his opponents with weights, Charles goaded them with pin-pricks. Instead of justifying oppression with administrative competence and military success, he exacerbated it with administrative failure and military defeat.

The pockets of the gentry and merchants were pillaged by the exaction of various arbitrary dues, such as Ship Money, which the King levied in default of regular supplies obtained by consent of Parliament, and the pride of the gentry was outraged through Laud's attempts to challenge their local authority by exalting that of the local Anglican incumbent. The Bible-reading piety of ordinary people all over the country—and it must never be forgotten that the English translation of the Bible was as much the text book of the Puritan revolution as *Das Kapital* was the text book of the Russian Revolution—was outraged by Laud's bureaucratic persistence in perverting the worship of God for the secular purposes of an ungodly State. Most important of all, the merchants of London, whose wealth and national importance had acquired for the City something of the prestige and autonomous privileges of a City State, were particularly affected by many of the expedients, such as the granting of monopolies and the levying of Tonnage and Poundage, adopted by Charles as a means of raising money, and particularly outraged by interference with their autonomy arising both from these taxes and from the censorship and other activities of Laud's Court of High Commission.

The secret both of the authority and of the aggressiveness of the Long Parliament lies first in the solid support which its leaders received from the semi-autonomous City of London, and secondly in the close connections which existed between the rich City merchants and the country gentry. The City of London, with its semi-autonomous Corporation, its city walls, its fortress, its train bands of City apprentices, its access to the sea and, above all, its easily negotiable wealth, was very much of an *imperium in imperio*. Within the shelter of its walls, citizens and allies could and did defy the King's will with impunity. It was only this solidarity of the City with the Long Parliament which enabled the Commons to bring Strafford and Laud, first to the Tower and then to the scaffold, and to break into pieces the whole machinery of Prerogative Courts and administrative acts with which the King had attempted to govern the country over the previous ten years.

This solidarity owed not a little to the close relationships between merchants and gentry which had grown up over the years and contemporaneously with the gradual emancipation both of the merchants and of the gentry from the influence and control of the feudal barons. Rich merchants were in the habit of buying country estates and themselves graduating into the ranks of the gentry. The younger sons of the gentry were frequently apprenticed to merchants and became, in due course, merchants themselves. There was much intermarriage between town and country. These close relations subsisted particularly between the City of London and the gentry of the Home Counties and East Anglia, and it is no accident that it was precisely these counties that proved, in the Civil War, to be the strongholds of the Parliamentary cause.

Later on, when internal dissensions, military reverses and defections to the Royalist cause were causing the City merchants to explore the possibilities of peace and compromise, it was the militant spirit of Puritanism which carried the matter to its victorious conclusion. But, for the years 1640-42, Puritan fervour was the servant rather than the master, the banner rather than the sword. But as the forces of self-interest, represented by the gentry and the City merchants, began to flag and fail when opposed to the loyalty which the name and office of King was still able to evoke, the fight was continued and won by the Puritan Elect, by the Saints and the Ironsides, who dwelt in a City not made with hands, and whose minds were fixed not on the fields of Hertfordshire and Kent, but on the green pastures of the Twenty-third Psalm.

The Puritanism of Pym and the leaders of the Long Parliament took the negative form of anti-clericalism. This arose from a natural fear of the Roman proclivities of the Court and from a natural reaction against the clerical excesses of Laud, and manifested itself principally in a determination to abolish Episcopacy, to prohibit the use of the Prayer Book, and to have a State Church controlled by a Commission of Laymen. This drab Erastianism, even more devoid of spiritual content than the ceremonial Erastianism of Laud, was far too secular a conception to take root in an essentially religious age, and its only result was to crystallize the diverse conceptions of Protestantism towards which Puritan England had been groping. On the right wing were those who were emotionally and doctrinally satisfied with the Prayer Book and with the Anglican Establishment generally, and who wished to avoid the two extremes of Erastianism (whether in the interest of King or Parliament) and clericalism (whether Anglican or Presbyterian), and who regarded sectarianism with the dislike of men to whom religious toleration was synonymous with political anarchy. When the Civil War broke out the Parliamentary representatives of this point of view were mostly to be found on the Royalist side, since this, for them, represented the lesser of two evils. In the centre were the Presbyterians who, until the Scottish alliance, derived their main support from the City of London. Presbyterianism was, in some sort, the logical consequence of an acceptance of the religious doctrines of the English Reformation, combined with a rejection of its political implications. The Presbyterian party gained the ascendancy in Parliament by means of the Scottish alliance and the signature of the Solemn League and Covenant, which pledged the support of Parliament for a Church Establishment in England 'according to the example of the best Reformed Churches', which, in the particular context of the Covenant, could reasonably be regarded as a pledge to impose Presbyterianism on England.

On the left wing were the Sectarians, the Zealots of English Puritanism. The Sectarians derived their strength and influence from those Bible-reading, psalm-singing, lay-preaching habits which formed the most deeply-rooted and most widespread manifestation of Puritanism in England, and which time has since shown to have represented the distinctive English twist taken by the movement of Reformation. In the event it was only the Sectarians who, in the crisis of the Civil War, had the religious fervour and the religious discipline to 'know what they were fighting for and to love what they knew', and to see the thing through to a successful conclusion. But the very qualities that enabled them to win a war, inhibited them afterwards either from co-operating with their friends or from conciliating their enemies. These inhibitions ensured both the failure of Puritan rule and the imperishability of the Puritan tradition.

The political failure of Puritanism was essentially a failure to relate the Puritan view of the nature of authority to the necessities of civil and religious administration. The war was won, and the climate of the revolution consequently conditioned, by the Puritan Sectarians. But their principles of toleration, and their successful fight for these principles, prevented them from applying these principles to those who did not themselves accept them. As these principles were in fact accepted by nobody except themselves, the triumph of such principles would have meant a dictatorship of the Saints. Such a dictatorship would have been, and, in so far as it was exercised, was a particularly oppressive one, since the Sectarian conception of toleration only applied to methods of worship and forms of government (and by no means completely even to these) and not at all to men's habits and customs.

In the event, the rigid insistence of the Sectarians on their principles immediately compelled Cromwell to hold the State together by the abandonment of principle and by recourse to expediency, and ultimately ensured the abandonment of principle altogether in the conduct of the English State. The effect of Cromwell's policy, forced on him by the Sectarians, was to destroy the principles of the Puritan Revolution, so far as the forms of government and the nature of authority were concerned, and to impose on the people at large the social peculiarities and prejudices of Puritanism, by way of compensation to the Sectarians for having deprived them of all real power. In this way Puritanism was politically frustrated and socially discredited.

Cromwell's claim to greatness is that, within the limitations set him by the people he had to deal with and the events with which he had to contend, he pursued a policy which, apart from restoring our national reputation abroad, saved England at home from the extremes of bloody repression and deepening chaos.

Cromwell neither betrayed, nor did he fulfil, the ideals of the Puritan Revolution. He tried and failed to make of Puritanism a political instrument. He was forced to acquiesce in an attempt, which failed, to impose upon England the Puritan pattern of social behaviour. But both these failures were contained within the frame of a larger success. A new principle of government had been asserted; a new standard of behaviour had been established. For good or ill the religious and secular principles of the Reformation had been consolidated, and were never again seriously to be challenged. The defeat of James II had been assured thirty years before he ascended the throne; England had been secured from the Counter-Reformation, and from all its implications of bloodshed, misery and obscurantism.

It was the religious fanaticism of the extremists on both sides which made the Civil War something greater than a mere episode in the struggle for power of a rising economic class. This religious fanaticism provided the fighting spirit and decided the issue. But the 'God with us' fervour of the victorious Sectarians was as much a minority movement under the Commonwealth as the 'Church and State' loyalty of the defeated Cavaliers was under the Restoration. Nevertheless it was this frustrated fervour and this long-suffering loyalty which gave an undertone of character and nobility to the succeeding age. Each of them, the one refusing religious and the other political conformity, in an age when men like Shaftesbury and Sunderland, Bolingbroke and Walpole, were typical representatives of England's rulers, became part of the heritage of England through persecutions endured, through evictions suffered, through blood shed, and through words of comfort and of treason whispered from mouth to mouth and from generation to generation, until, in the fullness of time, that which was thought could be boldly spoken, and that which was planned resolutely performed, to the greater glory of a people who had learnt the wisdom of toleration and the limitations of uniformity.

CHAPTER III

The Puritan Tradition in Religion

THE religious argument of the Reformation was an argument about the nature of authority. The medieval Church had made a tacit bargain with medieval man by which the Church relieved men of their personal responsibility towards God in return for obedience to the Church in matters of faith, doctrine and religious observance. The Protestants, in varying degrees and in various ways, asserted the personal responsibility of each individual man towards God. Having relieved the Church of its medieval obligation towards him, the Protestant naturally repudiated the Church's medieval claim on him.

The medieval Church claimed to be God's Representative on earth, and equated obedience to and faith in the Church with obedience to and faith in God. The validity of this claim was based on the doctrine of the Apostolic Succession by which the authority of the Apostles, as conferred on them by Our Lord, was transmitted to every priest of the Church by means of the laying on of hands in an unbroken chain of episcopal ordination stretching back through the mists of time to Our Lord's Charge to St. Peter.

Acceptance of the Church's claim was shaken partly by the Church's abuse of its authority, and partly by the development of national feelings which resented subordination to Rome over that large area of temporalities claimed by the Church as part of its domain. The influence of new intellectual ideas seems to have played little part in weakening the original allegiance, and appears to have come into play only during the subsequent process of seeking and building up alternative systems of authority.

In England the political break with Rome brought to the surface theories and questionings which had been maturing

27

quietly in country rectories and in University Colleges since the days of John Wyclif and the Lollards. After the necessity for strict doctrinal orthodoxy had departed with the death of Henry VIII, these theories and questionings spread with astonishing rapidity. The development of Reformist doctrines is attributable both to the contacts of dissident divines with Continental reformers during periods of exile under the Henrician and Marian persecutions, and to that intellectual vigour and ferment which was the precursor to the Elizabethan Age of Discovery. The spread of these doctrines was certainly attributable to the popularity of the English version of the Bible, which was now widely available and which seemed like a revelation to a still deeply religious people who had been starved of religious sustenance by the apathy and venality into which the majority of the clergy, both parochial and monastic, had fallen. The extent of this apathy and of this venality has been the subject of a great deal of controversy, much of which has not been remarkable for objectivity, but, even on the evidence of Roman Catholic apologists, there is no doubt at all that, in the first half of the sixteenth century, the Church in England had fallen into grave decadence, both as regards its monastic life and its parish priesthood.

In the Elizabethan settlement the Anglican Bishops aimed at an Establishment which would on the one hand take some account of the new thinking which the previous twenty years had released and on the other hand give sufficient authority to the Anglican Church to enable it to command the same temporal and spiritual obedience as had previously been claimed by and granted to Rome. For the political aim of the Reformation in England had been not only to sever the temporal and spiritual allegiance which bound Englishmen to Rome, but to transfer that allegiance from the Roman Pontiff to the English Crown. It is this conception of the Crown as being the inheritor of the loyalties previously owed to Rome which explains the insistence on religious uniformity exhibited both by the Tudors and by the Stuarts.

It was extremely difficult for the Anglican Bishops to reconcile the political necessity for maintaining the Church's authority

28

with the popular necessity for abandoning those ghostly claims which provided the basis and the justification for that authority. For the authority claimed by the Roman Church was based on, and sought its justification in, the peculiar access to and power of dispensing Divine Grace bestowed on it by the doctrine of the Apostolic Succession. And the religious theories of the Reformers were unmistakably based on a denial of the implications of that doctrine.

It is at this point that the Puritans come into English history. The Puritans were those who followed the implications of Reformist thought to their logical conclusion by accepting man's individual responsibility towards God and by rejecting the spiritual authority inherent in the institution of episcopacy. Their sense of individual responsibility towards God was manifested in their strict morals, in their habit of frequent prayer, in the sobriety of their clothes and of their behaviour, and, it must be added, in their tendency to self-righteousness and in their censoriousness towards other people. Their rejection of the apostolic conception of the priesthood implied by episcopal ordination was manifested in their refusal to accept the Order of Service as laid down in the Book of Common Prayer and the regulations regarding vestments and ornaments laid down by Archbishop Parker in his *Book of Advertisements*.

The Anglican Bishops, and probably a majority of the people of England, had no desire to follow matters to their logical conclusion. On the one hand national feeling, State policy, and a reaction against some of the abuses of the Roman system dictated a definite breach with Rome; on the other hand natural feeling was allied with State policy in a desire to preserve as much of the old ways and the old system of authority as was compatible with such a definite breach. In so far as Roman practices were admitted, they were admitted on grounds not of doctrine but of seemliness; in so far as episcopacy was justified (and it was in fact strenuously justified) it was justified on grounds of expediency and not with reference to the implications of the doctrine of the Apostolic Succession. (For example, Richard Hooker, defending episcopacy in his *Laws of Ecclesiastical Polity*,

29

explicitly states that 'no one form of Church government is prescribed as an immutable pattern by the Divine Word'.)

Almost from the beginning of Elizabeth's reign, two schools of thought are apparent in Puritanism. One school sought toleration for its practices outside the Church; the other school sought to convert the Church to its own way of thinking. The one tended to regard individual salvation as an end in itself, the other tended to regard it, at all events in part, as a means of influencing society. These two complementary strains will persist through the centuries, the one nourishing the other and between them making that massive contribution to English history which is the subject of this study.

During Elizabeth's reign the Queen and her Ministers and Bishops, by persecuting the Separatists and by disciplining the Nonconformists, were able for the most part to confine overt Puritan activity to the sphere of manners and morals. As a result the Puritans developed into a recognizable body in the kingdom, and particularly in the City of London. Morally the Puritans were representative of a sharp reaction against the prevailing Italianate licence which had become fashionable among the aristocracy and the intelligentsia, and which was the Transalpine Renaissance counterpart to the Northern European Reformist doctrines which formed the intellectual background of Puritanism. Socially the sober habit and consequent economic thriftiness of Puritans conformed well with the social ambitions and anti-aristocratic prejudices of the rising mercantile class who were beginning to take advantage of the new opportunities for enrichment afforded by the discoveries of the Navigators, by increased communication with Europe and by the supply of new money pouring into Europe from the New World beyond the Atlantic. It may well be that the aristocratic connotation of Episcopacy and the identification of the Established Church with an aristocratic State reinforced the theological beliefs of Puritanism.

In spite of the distaste which the manners and the morals of the Puritans must have provoked in an England where, in their various ways, aristocracy, intelligentsia and masses were reacting from medievalism in an access of sensual and almost pagan licence, they did in one great respect represent the spirit of the age. At a time when the emissaries of the Jesuits were doing their best to make Catholicism synonymous with treason, the Puritans were above suspicion on grounds of patriotism, since their anti-Catholic theology and their hatred of Spain (which was based on both theological and economic grounds) made them peculiarly representative of that aggressive English nationalism to which the Elizabethan Age gave rise.

The ambiguity of the Anglican Church on the doctrine of the Apostolic Succession, and the anti-Catholic feelings aroused by the treasonable activities of the Jesuits, made it possible, during Elizabeth's lifetime, for the majority of Puritans to remain within the Establishment in the hope of being able to influence the Establishment in the direction of their beliefs. Politically, too, the wise management by Elizabeth of her Parliaments—for example in the matter of monopolies—avoided the conscious formation of a common front against the Crown based on a determination to challenge the authority of the Crown both in doctrinal and in political matters.

This state of compromise came to an end at the Hampton Court Conference when James I, who shared the Puritan insistence on following modes of thought to their logical conclusion, linked the question of episcopacy with insistence on the absolute authority of the King by claiming that absolute authority as having been conferred by the act of anointing. The Stuart doctrine of the Divine Right of Kings, enunciated by James I and acted upon by Charles I, made it necessary for the Puritans to choose between exile or persecution on the one hand, and destroying the absolute power of the King on the other. It also gave birth to that alliance between Puritans and Parliament which was ultimately to bring Charles I to the block.

The Puritan-Parliament alliance had the effect of clarifying the basic difference between the Nonconformist and the Separatist Puritans. The Nonconformists agreed with the Anglicans in thinking in terms of a State Church and religious uniformity. They differed from the Anglicans in wanting a Church founded on Reformist principles, which involved a denial of all the

31

implications of belief in the Apostolic Succession. The political significance of Episcopacy, underlined by the Stuart Kings and their Bishops and Ministers, reinforced their theological objection to Episcopacy by political objection to the use of Episcopacy and its implications as a means of justifying the absolute authority of the Sovereign over the subject. The Separatists refused to acknowledge any spiritual or political authority as pertaining to the Church, which they regarded merely as a number of congregations of individual and like-minded worshippers. At that time the Separatists believed in toleration no more than did the Anglicans or the nonconformist Puritans, but they saw coercion not as the imposition of uniformity but as the denial to others of organizations and ceremonies not approved by themselves. If the Stuarts had pursued a more pliant policy, and if the menace of Catholic treason, on the decline since the execution of Mary Queen of Scots, had not fizzled out in the fiasco of the Gunpowder Plot, it is possible that nonconformist Puritan influence might have so impregnated the Establishment as to have brought about the evolution of a rigidly Protestant and uncompromisingly Erastian Church on much the same lines as the Scottish Presbyterian Establishment. This would have set English history on another and probably more authoritarian course.

As it was the centre of gravity of English Puritanism moved steadily from nonconformity to separatism until the 'reformation without tarrying for any' which had been adopted by extremist Puritan thought in Elizabeth's reign became the norm of English Puritan thought forty years later. This shift in the Puritan centre of gravity became increasingly apparent during the days of the Long Parliament until it issued in the domination of the Independents and in the expulsion of the Presbyterian majority from the Long Parliament.

There was no fundamental difference between the ideals of religious authority advocated by Presbyterians and Independents respectively. What had happened was that the Stuart persecutions had drawn so many Puritans so far along the road to separatism as to make it impossible for English Puritans as a whole to submit to the uniformity and discipline of Presbyterianism. They had become accustomed to minority thinking and were unable to adjust themselves to the discipline and organization necessary for a united national Church on the Presbyterian model. The 'sect-type' of Churchmanship was not so much the result of religious conviction as of 'minority' mentality. The development of 'sect-type' Churchmanship in Western Europe was conditioned not so much by differences in Christian belief, as by the amount of effective resistance offered by the State to the adoption of Reformist doctrines. In all Western European countries there certainly existed a 'lunatic fringe' of Puritan reformers who regarded separatism as a matter of principle but, for the main body of Puritans, in England as elsewhere, separatism was only adopted as a policy if and when it appeared to be an essential condition of persistence in the Reformed Faith. It is noteworthy that when the separatist Pilgrim Fathers settled in New England, they refused to recognize separatism when expressed in the form of deviation from their own beliefs, and persecuted those sects, such as the Quakers, who claimed that same right to liberty of worship for which the Pilgrim Fathers had become exiles.

We must now consider briefly the influence of Luther and Calvin respectively on English Puritanism, and the extent to which these influences tended to separate the Puritans from the Anglican Church and to encourage and perpetuate the separatism which Anglican persecution and Puritan fanaticism had precipitated.

The Lutheran doctrine of justification by Faith alone implied a view of Salvation as a definite, attainable and necessarily subjective state, which either had or had not been attained. The Calvinist doctrine of Predestination was a logical extension of the doctrine of justification by Faith alone. It was a matter of observation that some attained Salvation and that others did not. Since God was Omnipotent, the non-attainment of Salvation by some was part of the Will of God. Even though the attainment of Salvation through Faith might apparently be the result of the human will submitting itself to God, the activity of the human will was a function of an Omnipotent God. The observable fact that many people do not attain Salvation (on the assumption that

Salvation is a definite, attainable state) is either a derogation from God's Omnipotence or an acceptance of Predestination.

The Catholic view which, in spite of the apparent meaning of the Eleventh and Seventeenth Articles, was in practice adopted by the Anglican Church, consisted in the belief that Salvation was, not a definite state attainable on earth, but a progressive condition of relative nearness to or distance from God, a road along which all men could travel, and a road along which progress was assisted by the Sacraments of the Church and by works of Christian piety, motivated by Christian Faith. In terms of this belief the difference between a good man and a bad man was a difference not of kind but of degree, since they were not on opposite sides of a gulf, but at different stages along the same road.

The Continental Lutherans did not accept the logical Calvinist consequence of the doctrine of justification by Faith alone. The English Puritans, who did not accept the Calvinist position in toto, did, with some exceptions, and with much subsequent backsliding, accept the doctrine of Predestination. This fact does much to explain the later reaction towards secularism which did so much to undermine the Puritan tradition in England.

At the time of the outbreak of the Civil War, the doctrinal aspects of Royalist High Anglicanism on the one hand and of Parliamentary Presbyterianism on the other, had become inextricably involved with the political issue of whether authority in the State should be vested in the Crown or in Parliament. High Anglicanism had become the ecclesiastical counterpart of Royal absolutism, and Presbyterianism the religious expression of Parliamentary sovereignty. The loyalist fervour of the Catholics on the Cavalier right and the Puritanism of the Independents on the Parliamentary left alone gave a specifically religious aspect to the impending struggle. After the first stage of the Civil War, and so long as there appeared to be a possibility that Charles might be prepared to accept the reality of Parliamentary control, there seemed nothing much left for Anglicans and Presbyterians to quarrel about. In the Erastian climate created on each side by Laud and Pym respectively, the difference between Bishop and

Presbyter had almost narrowed down to one of nomenclature. But the untrustworthiness of Charles and the fanaticism of the Independents was to delay by twelve years the attainment of that secular compromise which was attained at the Restoration and which destroyed both in the English State and in the Anglican Church such roots of principle as still remained alive. But in these twelve years Puritanism, in the form of the Independent sects, although doomed, as part of the Restoration settlement, to political defeat, criminal persecution, and social obloquy, took sufficient root in the English soil as to make itself indestructible.

It is convenient at this point briefly to glance at the three main bodies into which Puritanism had become organized by the time of the Restoration.

First there were the Presbyterians, who consisted of those Puritans who wished for a State Church without Episcopacy or any form of sacerdotal or other appurtenances of belief in the Apostolic Succession, and whose doctrines, generally speaking, were expressed in the writings of Thomas Cartwright. The Presbyterians had gained control of the Establishment during the Long Parliament, and had made a political alliance, in the form of the Solemn League and Covenant, with the Scottish Presbyterian Church. This Presbyterian control of Church and State had been brought to an end by the victorious and predominantly Independent Army, and the Presbyterian majority in the Long Parliament expelled as a result of Pride's Purge in 1648. Under the Commonwealth the Presbyterians were represented on the Board of Triers and shared control of the Established Church with the Independent sects. Under the short lived rule of Richard Cromwell they regained their ascendancy, mainly as a result of General Monk's alliance with the Scottish Army, and were instrumental in arranging for the restoration of Charles II. Their efforts to secure a modified Presbyterianism under the Restoration failed and the Anglican Establishment restored by the Cavalier Parliament forced the Presbyterians into an undesired separatism and exposed them to the same régime of expulsions, deprivations, persecutions and disabilities as were suffered by the other Puritan bodies.

The Presbyterian outlook was based on being in control of a State Church or, at all events, of a Church in alliance with the State, and Presbyterian separatism was almost a contradiction in terms. Presbyterianism, during the hundred years from 1560 to 1660, largely derived from and was inspired by Presbyterian attempts to gain control of the Establishment. These attempts were finally frustrated by the Restoration and by the penal laws passed in defence of the reconstituted Episcopal Establishment, and from that time on English Presbyterianism withered and died.

The Congregationalists, who traced their descent from Robert Browne, the Elizabethan separatist and founder of the Browneite sect, formed the majority of the various sectarians who dominated Cromwell's New Model and gave the Puritan Revolution its distinctive colour. Like the Presbyterians, they were Calvinists, but unlike the Presbyterians they rejected the whole idea of a State Church in favour of separate congregations of believers deriving their authority direct from God. They had suffered persecution under Laud and many had gone into exile. (The Pilgrim Fathers were Congregationalists.) They opposed the Presbyterian Erastianism of the Long Parliament as resolutely as they had opposed the Anglican Erastianism of Laud.

The other important Independent body, the Baptists, like the Congregationalists, regarded religious organization in terms of 'gathered' congregations of believers deriving their authority direct from God. During the years of the Puritan Revolution they were allied with and politically indistinguishable from the Congregationalists and, like the Congregationalists, derived their main strength from the Army. In religious belief they were akin to the Congregationalists, but were distinguished from them by a disbelief in and a refusal to recognize or practise infant baptism, insisting on adult baptism as a conscious witness of Christian Faith and a condition of membership of the Baptist body. Both Baptists and Congregationalists held a perfectionist view of Salvation, although the Baptists held this less certainly than did the Congregationalists. (Indeed, if Baptism be regarded as a condition of Salvation it must, according to Puritan belief, be administered not as a means of bestowing Grace but as a conscious act of Faith which is obviously impossible for infants.) On the Calvinist belief in predestination the Baptists were divided; the General Baptists, spiritually descended from the Continental Anabaptists via John Smyth and Thomas Helwys, two English Puritan exiles who had come into contact with the Mennonite sect of Anabaptists in Holland, were Arminians; the Particular Baptists, who were an offshoot of Congregationalism, were Calvinists.

As Presbyterianism had triumphed over Anglicanism by reason of the support of the City of London and of the Scots, so the Independents triumphed over the Presbyterians by reason of the support of the Army. Having gained his political objectives by means of the Independents, and crushed the incipient alliance between the King and the Presbyterians, Cromwell imposed a religious truce within an Establishment comprising both Presbyterians and Independents, and imposed a political régime which acted independently of the predilections of either. The Independents, who lost much of their popular support and cohesion during the Commonwealth as a result of the fanaticism and extremism of some of the wilder Independent sects such as the Diggers and the Fifth Monarchy Men, could offer no collective resistance to the Restoration. But in the event, the expulsions and persecutions which followed affected them spiritually far less than they did the Presbyterians. The Independents were at home in separatism, whereas the Presbyterians were not.

Considering that Puritanism was distinguished by its refusal to subordinate religious convictions either to political expediency or to social convention, it is perhaps surprising that separatist— or as it is more popularly termed nonconformist—Puritanism was to become the seedbed not of religious revival but of materialist philosophy. The two great religious revivals of the eighteenth and nineteenth centuries—the Evangelical and the Oxford Movements—which quickened into life the embers of Christian Faith in England, each had its origin in Anglicanism. It was from the Evangelical Movement, inspired by John Wesley who was baptized into and died within the Anglican Communion, and not from its own resources, that nineteenth-century Puritanism drew such Christian inspiration as it possessed. Mr. R. H. Tawney in *Religion and the Rise of Capitalism* has traced the progress of Puritan transition from intense spirituality to no less intense materialism. It remains to examine the reasons underlying this, at first sight, strange metamorphosis. These reasons, it is suggested, inhere in some of the theological assumptions of the English Puritans.

The Puritans, by rejecting the conception of an authoritarian Church, rejected the conception of any authoritative and organized attempt to define and in some sort to impose a Christian code of behaviour in the ordinary transactions of life and, by so doing, to set limits to and to moderate the natural results of human acquisitiveness and human frailty. This function had, however imperfectly, been performed by the medieval Church, and was attempted by Laud through the machinery of the Court of High Commission. The Puritans, by rejecting the fetters of an imposed system of Christian belief, destroyed the discipline of an imposed system of Christian ethics, and attempted to substitute for it the individual fruits of Salvation as manifested by the Elect. In so doing they not only overestimated the influence of the minority of the Elect on the majority of the damned, but underestimated the corroding influence of Original Sin on the behaviour of the Elect. For the Puritan conception of the Salvation of the Elect seems to have assumed that the attainment of Salvation purged the Elect of any taint of Original Sin, by providing that the Divine Guidance to which the Elect had gained access was sufficient to offset the promptings of Original Sin. The inevitable effect of this view was that the Elect came to regard their works as providing their own justification instead of submitting these works to judgment in the light of the Faith by which alone they could be justified. For, by their rejection of outside authority, they had made of themselves judges of their own works, and, by their misconception of the nature of Salvation, had come to regard their own judgment as infallible.

This judgment was based on a personal interpretation of Holy Scripture, which was regarded as the literal Word of God.

It is difficult nowadays to appreciate the origin and, still more, the tenacity of the belief in the literal inspiration of the Bible—a belief which was by no means confined to the Puritans, and a belief which did more than anything else to impair the intellectual position of Christianity during the second half of the nineteenth century.

The Bible, when it became generally available in English, was popularly regarded as an authority on Divine matters superseding the authority of the Church. This status was acquired in view of the popularly felt need for an unimpeachable source of religious authority and in view of the Church's failure to satisfy that need. The Anglican Church never officially accepted the view that the Bible is the literal Word of God, and merely insisted on the necessity for Scriptural authority as the test of a Christian truth. (Sixth Article.) Hooker in his *Laws of Ecclesiastical Polity* made the point that it was the Church's function, in the light of tradition and in the light of its experience, to be the authoritative interpreter of Scripture. There are obvious possibilities of confusion in the Puritan habit of browsing through the Scriptures in search of a text to justify some act already motivated by individual judgment. There are obvious possibilities of error in a belief which places an equal, Divine, and literal value on the account of a tribal feud in the Arabian desert, on the verses of a sensual love poem, and on the dying words of the Redeemer of mankind.

There is some affinity between Puritan Christianity and Islam in their common belief in the literal inspiration of a Book. The origin of the belief was in both cases accompanied, and to some extent motivated, by a rejection of sacerdotalism, and has in both cases aborted the fruits of belief by inhibiting its development.

Towards the end of the eighteenth century belief in the literal inspiration of the Scriptures spread from Puritanism, via the Evangelical Movement, into the Anglican Church. As a result of this extension the scientific discoveries of the nineteenth century damaged the intellectual position of Christianity on a far wider front than would otherwise have been the case. But the most serious damage had been done long before the literal accuracy of the Bible had been impugned on scientific grounds in that belief in the literal inspiration of the Bible had provided the Puritans with a fatal facility for practising that vice of self-justification which was already inherent in the Puritan conception of Salvation.

In effect the supreme authority of Scripture interpreted by individual judgment proved unable adequately to Christianize the various potent manifestations of Puritan energy which, during the course of the eighteenth century, were diverted more and more into materialist channels.

This decline in the Christian vitality of Puritan Nonconformity can be seen both in the demoralizing effect of the climate of religious toleration and political disability under which the Non-conformists lived during the eighteenth century, and in the deadening effect of a 'Religion of the Book', which subjected Christian truth to the rationalist limitations of eighteenth-century thought.

The intellectual ability, energy and application of the Puritans inevitably raised many of them to positions of wealth and influence, in which they found that their legitimate ambitions for social advancement, municipal office and political places were denied them as a result of their religious beliefs. They were therefore faced individually with the temptation of compromising with their beliefs either by the practice of 'occasional conformity' or (when this was forbidden) by abandoning altogether the public expression of these beliefs. Corporatively they were faced with the temptation of subordinating the religious observances of their sects to the political function of endeavouring to remove the disabilities under which they suffered. These temptations were not wholly resisted; on the one hand the number of Nonconformists steadily declined as a result of reabsorptions into the Anglican Church; on the other hand Nonconformity tended to become less and less of a religious movement and more and more of a political lobby operating in the murky atmosphere of eighteenth-century corruption and intrigue.

On the religious plane the errancy of human judgment, un-informed and uncontrolled by an objective body of authority, exposed Puritan Christianity to three different trends of materialist heresy.

Humanism. There is abundant evidence that in many Nonconformist congregations the stern requirements of Puritan theology became gradually eroded until a type of Christianity was taught and followed which involved nothing much more than following the dictates of one's conscience and 'leading a decent life'. This was partly the result of whittling away doctrinal requirements in order to avoid dissension and secession.

Unitarianism. The denial of the doctrine of the Trinity, on the ground that no specific justification for this doctrine can be found in the New Testament (Unitarian theologians, who were not alone in their belief, proved to their satisfaction that I John v. 7 was a forgery), in effect led to a denial of the Divinity of Christ and placed Unitarians outside the limits of Christianity. The original Unitarian Churches, all of which were derived from seceding Nonconformist congregations (Presbyterian congregations were affected to such an extent that for some time, in England, the expressions Presbyterian and Unitarian were almost interchangeable), were the outward and visible forms taken by such eighteenth century agnosticism as was not yet sufficiently 'emancipated' from its Christian antecedents to deny Christianity altogether. Unitarianism was of course no new thing. Under the name of Socinianism (punishable by death under the Long Parliament) it had existed as a heresy both in Europe and in England since the sixteenth century; but its organization into 'Churches' in England dates from the eighteenth century only.

Antinomianism. This was a particular heresy of Calvinism, by which Election to Salvation was deemed as releasing the Elect from what were generally regarded as the obligations of Christian morality and conduct. It is a feature of English Antinomianism, and an interesting comment on the deep ethical influence of Puritanism, even when divorced from its religious content, that this heresy was not to any large extent exhibited in licentious conduct. Antinomians seemed to have been more concerned with the intellectual justification of licentiousness than with its actual practice.

The Society of Friends, the *ne plus ultra* of Puritan thought and practice, has some claim to be regarded as an exception to this process of decline. The Quakers were distinguished from the main body of Nonconformist Puritanism in that they took their stand, not on the literal inspiration of the Bible, but on direct communion with God. At the expense of continual secession which severely limited both their numbers and their influence, the Quakers did preserve in practice the original Puritan ideal of Faith issuing in works which were justified not by an appeal to individual judgment nor by the authority of a Biblical text but by a continual reference to the Divine source of Faith. The Quakers really did see and guard against, as the generality of Puritans did not, the dangers of arrogance issuing from a system in which every man was his own priest, and the dangers of wealth which, in an expanding economy, was the frequent outcome of Puritan habits of self-restraint, application, and self-denial. But the principles and practices of Quakerism were too heroic to make much appeal to the ordinary man, and the development of Quakerism took place somewhat outside the main stream of English Puritanism. But even the Quakers did not remain entirely unaffected by the Zeitgeist of the eighteenth century, although their reaction to it was one of quietism rather than materialism.

An element which was curiously lacking in the religion both of the Anglican Establishment and of the Nonconformist Churches and Congregations between the Reformation and the Wesleyan Revival was the element of compassion. On the Anglican side the burnings of the sixteenth century, the imprisonments and deprivations of the seventeenth, and the disdainful toleration of the eighteenth centuries were all equally devoid of any element remotely akin to the compassionate Spirit of Jesus. On the Puritan side this element was similarly lacking in the anti-episcopal diatribes of Cartwright, in the religious ecstasies of the Independent 'Saints', and in the sober righteousness of the eighteenth century Nonconformists. As far as the Puritans are concerned this lack of compassion is explained partly by their individual, almost solitary, conception of a man's duty towards his God, partly by the theoretical other-worldliness which seems to have been adopted as a sort of defence mechanism in compensation for the practical worldliness practised by their unregenerate natures, and partly by the Calvinist belief in Predestination which held that the world 'is disposed for the best by a Power of which they are the humble instruments'.

Theologically English Puritanism derived about equally from the doctrines of Luther and the doctrines of Calvin. If the belief in Predestination was characteristically Calvinist, the individual and solitary conception of man's relationship with God was characteristically Lutheran. 'God speaks to the soul, not through the mediation of the priesthood or of social institutions built up by man, but *solus cum solo*, as a voice in the heart and the heart alone. Thus the bridge between the world of spirit and the world of sense is broken and the soul is isolated from the society of men that it may enter into communion with its Maker. The Grace that is freely bestowed on it may overflow in its social relations, but these relations can supply no particle of spiritual nourishment to make easier the reception of Grace' (Tawney). It would be difficult to find a better description of the strength and weakness of English Puritan religion. This Lutheran quietism (of which the history of German Protestantism provides such a melancholy illustration), combined with the Calvinist belief in Predestination and the corruption of individual human judgment unsustained by any external props in the form of tradition or of organization, inevitably resulted in Puritan thinking being dominated by the conception of man's duty towards God to the virtual exclusion of his duty towards his neighbour. Also, belief in the literal inspiration of the Bible, by attaching equal importance to the Old as to the New Testament, aided this tendency by minimizing the relative importance of such passages as the Parable of the Samaritan and by maximizing the importance of the success stories of Abraham, Joseph and David as compared with the obscure life and shameful earthly end of the Incarnate Son of God.

As a result of the anti-social attitude both of the Anglican Establishment which was, almost by definition, wedded to the *status quo*, and of the Nonconformists, it came about that eighteenth-century humanitarianism was not only irreligious but specifically anti-Christian. In so far as Puritans were associated with this humanitarianism—and they were largely associated with it—they only became associated with it to the extent that they detached themselves from their original religious beliefs.

It was due mainly to Methodism, and to the Evangelical Revival, that English Christianity began once more to recognize in theory and in practice that this world is also part of God's Kingdom, and to re-assert, and perhaps even to over-emphasize, that element of compassion which led to the Christian fruits of the nineteenth and twentieth centuries.

Methodism introduced a new stream of vitality into Nonconformity just as the Evangelical Revival introduced a new stream of vitality into the Establishment. It is necessary to consider the relation between Nonconformist Puritanism and Methodism and between Methodism and Evangelicalism in order to assess the influence on the Puritan tradition of the religious revival which embraced both Evangelicalism and Methodism.

We have seen that sixteenth-century Puritanism, in its religious aspect, derived from a revolt against the implications of the doctrine of the Apostolic Succession, and was characterized by a belief in a perfectionist doctrine of Salvation, in the sovereignty of individual judgment, in the literal inspiration of the Bible and in Predestination. It rose to power as the result of a successful political struggle against the religious discipline of the Establishment, it fell from power as the result of the restoration of that discipline, and it maintained itself in being throughout the years of deprivation (active persecution ceased after 1690) by a continued insistence on the beliefs which had brought them into power.

Methodism was primarily a revolt against the apathy of the Establishment and the materialism of society. There was no doctrinal or political quarrel either with the Establishment or with society, and Methodist influence developed as a result not of political action but of the preaching of Wesley and his companions. Listening to sermons played the same role in Methodism as Bible-reading had played in the early days of Puritanism.

Puritans and Methodists had the same conception of Salvation as an attainable perfectionist state. The Puritans conceived it as attained slowly by means of intellectual struggle, the Methodists as attained suddenly by means of emotional ecstasy. (The Wesleyan technique of emotional and sudden conversion was to have a considerable influence on Anglo-Saxon Christianity.) The Puritans of course had their lunatic fringe of emotional enthusiasts, but 'enthusiasm' in the pejorative eighteenth-century sense was never a characteristic of Puritanism as it was of Methodism.

The Puritans insisted on taking their denial of the doctrine of Apostolic Succession to its logical conclusions; the Methodists were apt to shy away from the intellectual and political implications of their religious attitudes. Puritanism and Methodism were both based on an individual approach to God, without the intermediary of a priest. The Puritans sought to approach God through the Holy Spirit as revealed in Scripture, the Methodists through Jesus Christ as revealed to the human heart. Puritanism was the religion of the saving Grace of the Holy Spirit; Methodism was the religion of the redeeming Blood of Jesus. Puritanism is illustrated by the hymns of John Bunyan, Methodism by the hymns of Charles Wesley. Puritanism tended to repel people by the ease with which one was damned, Methodism by the ease with which one could be saved.

But, with all these differences, Puritanism and Methodism produced the same fruits of sober living, hard working, thrift, and strict Sabbath observance. Methodism affected the other Nonconformist Churches as a stimulant, invigorating and profoundly changing their beliefs and practices. The Methodists themselves at first occupied a position midway between the Establishment and the older Nonconformists, and were distinguished from them by their abstention from the Radical and Reformist politics with which the older Nonconformists identified themselves during the first half of the nineteenth century. But in time, and particularly as the influence of the Oxford Movement made itself felt in the Establishment, the Methodists tended to draw away from the Establishment and towards the older Nonconformists until, by the end of the nineteenth century, the 'Free Churches' or the 'Nonconformist vote' presented to the world a united front of Liberal politics and austere morals stretching from the Quakers on the left to the Wesleyan Methodists on the right.

The Evangelical Revival brought Puritanism back into the Establishment for the first time since it had been driven out by the Stuart persecutions. It is a moot point whether Methodism and the Evangelical Revival were two parallel but independent reactions from eighteenth-century apathy and agnosticism or whether the Evangelical Revival derived from the teachings of Methodism. It was certainly influenced by Methodism; but it was distinguished at many points and developed quite differently from Methodism although, at the outset, opponents referred to Evangelicals and Wesleyans impartially as Methodists. Both movements were influenced and to some extent inspired by the works of William Law, and particularly by his 'Serious Call', in that Law was the first really important and influential writer to ground a case for personal piety and devotion on the theology of the Anglican Establishment. Until Law started publishing his works Anglican writers had concentrated, first on a defence of the doctrinal position of Anglicanism *vis-à-vis* Rome on the one hand and Calvinism and Lutheranism on the other, and later, with the spread of Socinian doctrines, on a defence of Trinitarian Christianity. The acceptance of the Anglican doctrinal position (with the exception of the doctrine of Apostolic Succession on which Anglicanism was equivocal) by both Evangelicals and Methodists is evidence of the influence of these divines in consolidating the intellectual and doctrinal position of the Establishment. But the keynote of both movements, personal piety and devotion, derived from faith and expressed in works, was influenced partly by the example of the Puritans (and in Wesley's case to a very large extent by the example of the Lutheran Moravians) and partly by the writings of Law. Neither movement followed the Puritan example, either politically or theologically, of rejecting the theory of a State Church in general or the practices of the Anglican Church in particular. The ultimate secession of the Methodists was caused, first by the practice of itineracy, and secondly by Wesley's ordination of his own clergy. Neither of these developments was a matter of doctrine, and each was brought about as a result of the inadequacy of the Anglican machinery to cater either for the new urban populations brought into being in England by industrialization or for the scattered populations in the North American colonies. The Evangelical Movement, which was principally addressed to the upper and middle classes, while Wesley was avowedly and deliberately addressing himself to the masses, was faced with no such problems and consequently with no such temptations to quarrel with the Establishment.

The Methodists took little or no part in contemporary political or social movements. The Evangelicals, feeling acutely the responsibilities of wealth, intellect and influence, devoted themselves to humanitarian, social and missionary work. At the same time they actively opposed most aspects of the Radical policies supported by the Freethinkers and older Nonconformists; they saw social justice not as a human right to be extorted from the rich but as a human dignity to be bestowed by the rich.

The permanent influence of the Methodists lay primarily in the revitalization of those Dissenting communities which had been driven into Nonconformity at the Restoration and which developed independently of the Establishment after the Restoration. Methodism re-christianized a way of life which was becoming more and more influenced by materialism as a result of the struggle for political liberty and social betterment imposed by the disabilities suffered by Nonconformists during the eighteenth century.

The Evangelicals were enabled, by the religious toleration of the age, to play within the Establishment the role which might have been played by the Puritans a century and a half before. They restored to the Anglican laity a tradition of personal devotion, sober living and charitable activity. They prevented the Anglican Church from becoming a sect by narrowing the social and doctrinal gap between the Establishment and Non-conformity in the same way as the Oxford Movement was to narrow the social and doctrinal gap between the Establishment and Rome. But the Evangelical Movement seems to have had within it those same materializing and secularizing influences as were inherent in the early Puritan movement. The Evangelicals did not, like the Puritans, deny the authority of the Church, but their beliefs prevented them from feeling any confidence in the authority which they conventionally accepted.

The influence of Methodism reinvigorated and at the same time profoundly changed the character and outlook of Nonconformist Puritanism. Evangelizing rather than theology became the principal note of the movement. This temporarily reasserted the Christian influence of Nonconformity, but permanently impaired its intellectual content. The hard, self-contained, intellectual, Calvinist discipline which the Nonconformist Puritans, in spite of all their eighteenth-century aberrations, had in some measure preserved from their seventeenth-century inheritance, was imperceptibly softened by the influence of Methodism into a religion suitable for teaching to the semi-barbarous masses in the new industrial towns of England and to the wholly barbarous masses of Africa and the Indies. The sturdy self-sufficiency which in the eighteenth century had financed and maintained the Dissenting Academies was diverted into a growing demand for a system of State-aided and non-denominational (which in practice meant secular) system of education. The free-will offerings which had been previously devoted to the self-improvement of the Nonconformists themselves were devoted more and more to evangelical and missionary work. The political emphasis on a removal of the disabilities affecting the Nonconformists was diverted, as a result of the gradual removal of these disabilities, into a demand for social justice for the working class as a whole, of whom the Nonconformists, as a result of Methodist evangelism, made up a considerable part. The Nonconformist vote, which became important after the passage of the Reform Bill in 1832, and increasingly important after the passage of subsequent Reform Bills, was used less to promote the influence of the

Nonconformists as such than to seek benefits for those classes in which Nonconformity was increasingly represented.

This broadening of Nonconformist interests was caused partly by the evangelizing influence of Methodism, partly by the removal of the disabilities affecting Nonconformists, and partly by the progressive extensions of the vote which gave the franchise to thousands of previously unenfranchised Nonconformists.

It is difficult to say whether the decline of Calvinist beliefs was a result or an additional cause of this broadening of interests. The Methodists, following the example of John Wesley, for the most part rejected Predestination. (Those who followed White-field's lead and accepted Predestination either joined the Countess of Huntingdon's Connexion or became identified with the Evangelical wing of the Establishment.) This, together with the influence of the General Baptists, who also rejected Predestination, had the effect of gradually sapping the influence of Calvinist theology from the whole body of English Nonconformity. This conviction of being one of the Elect had, more than anything else, given to English Puritanism its characteristic features—its self-reliance, its endurance under persecution, its intellectual arrogance, its lack of human sympathy, its concentration on self-improvement and its indifference to social justice for others. Even in the midst of the Puritan aberrations of the first half of the eighteenth century Puritan Calvinism, while it failed to preserve the original Christian impulse of Puritanism, and while it failed in a theological sense to retain its hold on Puritan congregations, secured and strengthened, in a society notable for the laxity of its personal and commercial morals, the traditional Puritan virtues of sobriety, application and probity. The decline of Calvinist beliefs among the Nonconformist bodies heightened their social and religious sympathies and quickened their evangelical enthusiasm. But at the same time it lowered their intellectual standards and blunted their emphasis on self-reliance. State aid rather than self-help began to become the secular note of Nonconformity just as the Compassion of Jesus rather than the Omnipotence of God became the dominating religious note.

These new notes in Nonconformity meant in effect that the

centre of gravity of the Puritan tradition passed away from the Separatists and back into the Anglican Church, where the Evangelical Movement, uncompromisingly Calvinist and sternly individualist, inherited, more nearly than the post-Wesleyan Nonconformists, the limitations and virtues of English Puritanism.

In the short run the intellectual limitations, the Erastian sympathies and the Conservative politics of the Evangelicals appeared to inhibit the religious and social effects of their Puritan beliefs; but in the long run the Evangelicals, precisely because of these limitations, were able to do what the Nonconformists had never been able and would never have been able to do; they wove Puritanism, as a permanent and indestructible strand into the very fabric of English life.

We have described the Evangelical Movement as bringing Puritanism back into the Establishment. Certainly the prevailing external tone of the Anglican middle class during the nineteenth century, with its insistence on the virtue of hard work and the vice of idleness, its Sunday observance, its self-reliance, its thrift and its intolerance of the 'pleasant vices', was reminiscent of many of the aspects of sixteenth- and seventeenth-century Puritanism. To what extent was this due to a continuity of religious principle? Can the sober characteristics of the Victorian middle class be regarded as being in the true line of descent of the Puritan tradition? It is necessary to show both the congruence of Evangelicalism with religious Puritanism and the connection of Evangelicalism with Victorian middle-class morality.

Two characteristic notes of Puritanism were a rejection of the Sacraments of the Church and an assertion of personal communion with the Holy Spirit as the principal means of Grace, together with rejection of doctrinal conformity and an assertion of personal obedience to God as a necessity of the good life. These notes accorded with the Evangelical view both of the Sacraments (which they regarded as being of much less importance than did the Methodists) and of the necessity for a devout personal life. The Evangelical view of the Church was much the same as that of the Presbyterians, except that the Evangelicals believed in toleration and the Presbyterians did not; both believed in a State Church with its authority derived not from the Apostolic Succession but from the law of the land. Both accepted the doctrine of Predestination and consequently the perfectionist nature of Salvation. (Here again the Evangelicals were more congruent with the Puritans than with the Methodists.) Both believed in the literal inspiration of the Bible and in the superiority of that inspiration to the doctrine of the Church (a fact which was to have unfortunate results both for the Evangelicals and for the Anglican Church), and above all they both believed in the supreme importance of the human will as a means of achieving and maintaining access to the Holy Spirit of God.

The importance of the human will in the practice of the Christian religion and in the conduct of earthly life is the supreme characteristic of English Puritanism. (Paradoxically, belief in Predestination only served to increase the Puritan sense of the importance of the human will of the Elect as being the chosen instrument of God for the fulfilment of His Purposes on earth.) It is this emphasis on the human will which provides the key to the spiritual weakness and the moral strength of the Puritan contribution to English life. The Methodist conception of God seeking man through the redeeming Blood of Jesus is almost as absent from traditional Puritanism as is the Catholic conception of God being available to man through the Sacraments of the Church. The supreme ecstasy of one who, while seeking, realizes that he is being sought, savours almost of blasphemy to the true Puritan.

It is this emphasis on the human will which provides the strongest and most obvious link between the Puritan Independent of the seventeenth century and the Victorian Evangelical of the nineteenth and which enabled each of them to make an indelible mark of iron on the age in which he lived.

The fashionable agnostic doctrines of the eighteenth century received a sharp set-back in polite society in England when former sympathizers saw these same doctrines ripen into the bloody harvest of Jacobinism on the other side of the Channel. The staunch Conservatism of the Evangelicals (who set their faces hard against Trade Unionism and any agitation among the masses) and the emollient influence of Methodism among the workers, in whom Christian meekness was an especially seasonable virtue during the first half of the nineteenth century, caused a revulsion of feeling in favour of Christianity among the English upper class. Of this reaction Evangelicalism, as being the most active and most influential contemporary movement in the Church, was the principal beneficiary. Evangelical Christianity became not only socially respectable; it became fashionable. But its intellectual status never approached its social eminence; consequently its influence declined as the social reasons for its popularity receded. At the same time, as had been the case with the early Puritans, the secular habits of the Evangelicals, conforming as they did with the economic needs and climate of the times, persisted long after their religious inspiration had departed.

Evangelicalism, although it numbered among its leaders, both clerics and laymen, a large number of educated and intelligent people, was never an intellectual movement. It was in some sort a reaction against the agnostic intellectualism of the eighteenth century. One can discern in the movement a sort of perverse pride in abandoning the intellect on the threshold of religion, a determination to exclude the human reason from communion with God, instead of calling upon God to supplement the deficiencies of human reason.

Puritan beliefs were fashioned at a time when men's minds were still under the domination of the Age of Faith. The miraculous pretensions of the Church were rejected not because of their improbability but because of their abuse. The literal inspiration of the Bible, the existence of special Providences, the reality of hell fire and an anthropomorphic conception of heaven were believed in because such beliefs were congruent with the thought of an age in which intelligent men believed in witchcraft and in the efficacy of charms and curses. The Evangelicals had no such intellectual excuse for almost similar beliefs after two centuries of uninhibited thought and scientific discovery. While early Puritan beliefs were in accordance with, Evangelical beliefs were in conscious and deliberate opposition to, the intellectual and scientific climate of the age.

The Evangelical movement was the channel through which Puritanism was injected into the English social life of the nineteenth century. It was not the principal means by which this Puritanism was manifested. For, as in the seventeenth and eighteenth centuries, we find that Puritanism had dug far deeper roots and spread far wider branches than would have seemed possible from an inspection of the original plant.

The particular social significance of the Evangelical movement was that it set the fashion for a Christian standard of behaviour at or near the top of society from which it worked downwards, at the same time as the Methodists were inculcating a Christian standard of behaviour at or near the bottom of society from which it worked upwards. In both cases the specifically religious doctrines which had inspired this standard of behaviour were abandoned by the generality of people who accepted the standards which derived from them. But these doctrines did profoundly if unconsciously influence the social outlook of the English people. The Arminian influence of Methodism caused Nonconformity as a whole to identify itself with those Liberal policies and with that secular outlook which assumed the innate goodness of man and which assumed that most social evils could be removed as a result of education, persuasion and legislation. The Calvinist belief of the Evangelicals, on the other hand, coincided with the prejudices of the upper and middle class to create a new Conservative tradition in which material happiness was not a human right but the due reward of application, and in which social justice was regarded as being a result of the altruism of the few rather than of the organized self-interest of the many.

It is on the rock of Calvinism that the Puritan tradition split. The Arminians—which meant in practice most of the post-Wesleyan Nonconformists—joined the eighteenth-century Radicals to form the great stream of the Liberal tradition. The Calvinists gave a social content to English Conservatism by equating the godliness of the Elect with social privilege and material fortune and, in so doing, by imposing on privilege and fortune the sense of responsibility expected from the Elect.

According to this argument, Calvinism, secularized into a

theory of sanctified and responsible privilege, is an essential element in the Puritan tradition, and provides the touchstone by which the legitimate descendants of the Puritan tradition may be recognized. If this argument be accepted the main stream of nineteenth-century Nonconformity passes out of the Puritan and into the Liberal tradition, and the Established Church, while not itself entering into the Puritan tradition, becomes the medium through which the Puritan tradition is filtered into English society from above.

The doctrine of Predestination was not brought into the Establishment by the Evangelicals. Although Laud had given the Establishment an Arminian flavour, the Anglican Church had not, in its Articles, by any means repudiated the doctrine of Predestination. On the contrary, the Seventeenth Article specific-ally accepts it, and the tone of eighteenth-century Anglican theologians is on the whole mildly Calvinist. It may plausibly be argued that the Anglican Church has been particularly addicted to a kind of Calvinist heresy (not dissimilar to Antinomianism) by which social inequalities have been justified and sanctified by equating social inequality with Divine Election. It was the particular service of nineteenth-century Puritanism that it carried this heresy to its logical conclusion by insisting on the beneficiaries of social inequality trying to behave as if this heresy were the truth.

The Evangelical movement proved unable—as far as the generality of men were concerned—to give any continuing spiritual inspiration to the ethical standards which they had introduced into English society. This was due partly to the intellectual contradictions inherent in the movement, which gave authority to a Church which they had divested in advance of any Divine Source of authority. By their denial of Sacramentalism they denied men the concept of offering back to God that which they had received as a result of their Faith in God. By their appeal over the head of the Church to the literal authority of Scripture they inhibited the Church from its function of interpreting Scripture. They failed to provide, or rather they did not see that it was the function of the Church to provide, for the continual renewal of God's Grace in the heart of man. By denying the function of the Altar as a Place of Sacrifice, they allowed men to erect their own altars to sacrifice to gods of their own choosing. Their system of theology was inadequate to appeal to men's heads; their system of worship was inadequate to appeal to men's hearts. As in the eighteenth, so in the nineteenth century, Puritanism failed as a religion because of its failure to create and to sustain a continuing authority and tradition within which the Puritan concept of man's personal responsibility to God could be exercised. Puritanism liberated great and beneficent energies in man without providing the spiritual means by which he could use these energies for the greater glory of God.

The gradual loss of any specific spiritual content meant that nineteenth-century Puritanism ceased to have any specific connection with any recognizable group of people, but became instead an impalpable, intangible, but none the less potent, although mainly secular, influence throughout the whole of English society.

The failure of Puritan religious principles permanently to establish themselves either within the Anglican Church or in Nonconformist circles should not be allowed to obscure the powerful indirect influence of Puritanism on English religious practice. At the time of the Reformation the connection between personal piety and religious belief had practically ceased to exist either among the clergy or among the laity. The fruits of Faith were regarded almost entirely in terms of obedience to the doctrines and observances of the Church and hardly at all in terms of a personal attempt to follow the precepts and to imitate the example of Christ. The clergy were corrupted by power and the laity by irresponsibility and both, as a result of this corruption, tended to commute the obligations of the Christian life into the outward observance of standardized Christian forms. The practice of buying and selling Indulgences is an extreme example of this corruption as it affected both clergy and laity.

Puritanism was responsible for re-establishing in England the connection between personal piety and religious observance. The fact that this connection is not an inevitable one is apparent from even a cursory glance at clerical circles in Roman Catholic countries to-day. The fact that the appearance of personal piety became, as a result of Puritan influence, a socially necessary concomitant of religious observance may account both for the accusation of hypocrisy frequently levelled against Puritans and for the identification between licentiousness and unbelief which grew up during the nineteenth century. (This identification, which may seem apparent to most Protestants, was by no means self-apparent in England before the nineteenth century, and is by no means self-apparent in most Roman Catholic countries to-day.)

There is plenty of apathy and worldliness among both Anglican and Nonconformist clergy; but at least this apathy and worldliness are regarded as derogatory to their professions. There is no doubt some licentiousness in exceptional cases; but at least this licentiousness is regarded as disqualifying culprits from the exercise of their profession. Among the laity the profession of religious belief, if it has not acted powerfully as an inspiration to righteousness, has at least served as a brake on wrongdoing. At worst, church-people have assumed a virtue if they had it not, and it is reasonable to suppose that this assumption not only cloaks, but to some extent hinders, the practice of vice.

That connection between religious observance and active benevolence, which is characteristic of the Quakers, which was characteristic of the Evangelicals, and which is now generally established in England as a necessary condition of the Christian life, cannot be regarded as being specifically due to Puritan influence. The Puritan insistence on personal piety tended to overlay the emphasis placed by the medieval Church on benevolence with the result that post-Reformation 'good works' had their origin mostly from outside organized Christianity until the Evangelicals revived the old tradition. The great upsurge of missionary endeavour at the beginning of the nineteenth century was due mainly to Methodist influence, although it was brought into and powerfully developed within the Anglican Church by the Evangelicals.

In sum, the two great streams of Christian tradition in England

—the Sacramental and the Evangelical—which make up the Anglican heritage, are neither specifically Puritan. The Evangelical movement, although inheriting and carrying on the Puritan tradition in religion was, in many of its most virile aspects, and particularly in its social and missionary work, outside the Puritan tradition. English religious life was permanently affected by Puritanism only to the extent that English life as a whole was so affected. Puritanism bestowed on English religious life, as it bestowed on English secular life, those qualities deriving from a belief in Original Sin and from a belief in Divine Election which, by means of the Holy Spirit operating on the human will, is able to redeem the Elect from the consequences of Original Sin and to endow them with the capacity for demonstrating their Divine Election in the labours of their earthly lives. In consequence, the fruits of Puritanism, in secular as in religious life, were an acute sense of personal responsibility, an immense application, an iron will, a sober realization of the vice of idleness and the folly of waste, together with a strong tendency towards self-justification and self-righteousness.

CHAPTER IV

The Puritan Tradition in Politics

PURITANISM was a religious movement; its secular attitudes derived from its religious attitudes and not *vice versa*. Its religious note was a rejection of the traditional authority of the Church; its corresponding secular note was a rejection of the traditional authority of the State. Those who complain nowadays of the all-embracing tentacles of the modern State are apt to forget the tremendous authority and no less tremendous responsibility claimed and effectively exercised by the State in Tudor times. The *laissez faire* attitude adopted by the State during the eighteenth and early nineteenth centuries towards social questions and towards problems of production and distribution was due to the Puritan-inspired breaking up of the comprehensive apparatus of State control built up by such men as Thomas Cromwell, Walsingham and Strafford. The limitations on the rebuilding and the conditions imposed on the functioning of that apparatus during the last 100 years (a rebuilding necessitated by the chaotic social consequences of unadulterated *laissez faire*) derive mainly from the individualist ideas inherited from the Puritan Revolution.

Puritan dislike of State interference, which started as the secular aspect of Puritan religious belief, was sustained partly by a desire to limit the power and will of the State to impose religious uniformity and partly by a desire to limit State interference with commercial enterprise. (The medieval State, as a matter of course, controlled 'private enterprise' to a far greater extent than the Labour Party to-day have even contemplated.) The adventitious alliance between Puritanism and Parliament during the first half of the seventeenth century resulted temporarily (during the life of the Long Parliament) in an attempt, not to limit State control, but to transfer that control from the Crown

to Parliament. This was the secular corollary of the attempt by
the Long Parliament to obtain control of the Established Church.
Both these attempts failed, partly because of the administrative
inexperience and incapacity of the Long Parliament (which acted
both as a legislative assembly and as an autocratic government)
and partly because of the unashamedly predatory and tyrannical
notions of the Presbyterian majority in the Long Parliament.
The Independent Puritans reacted against Presbyterian domination with the same violence and with the same success as the
Presbyterians had reacted against the domination of the Crown.
But the very nature of Puritan beliefs—both religious and secular
—condemned them to perpetual, although sometimes effective,
opposition in any organized State. The Rule of the Saints is not
a practicable ideal. After their victory over the Long Parliament,
and always thereafter, the Puritan tradition in politics was to
limit the power of the State to interfere with the individual.
During the second half of the seventeenth and the first half of the
eighteenth centuries this attempted limitation was mainly concerned with the removal of political and social disabilities affecting
Dissenters; thereafter, the dispute between individualism and
State control tended to concentrate on resistance to legislation
imposing State control of trade and employment and State
financing of social services.

The steady movement towards the conception of a State
which, in Lord Melbourne's words, existed merely 'to prevent
crime and to preserve contracts' was made possible, first by the
destruction of the Court of High Commission and the Court of
Star Chamber and other appurtenances of State control, and
secondly by the attainment, after the Restoration, of a balance
between Parliament and the Executive which prevented on the
one hand the usurpation by Parliament of the powers previously
wielded by the Crown and on the other hand the reconstruction
by the Crown of the authoritarian machinery perfected by the
Tudors and early Stuarts. When in course of time the authority
of the State was restored as a result of the majority in Parliament
becoming the automatic register of the will of the Party in
power, the advent of universal suffrage maintained the precarious

balance by making the authority of the Government dependent on the approval of a popular majority. The fact that in practice this often amounted merely to the substitution of small scale bribes to Members of Parliament by large scale promises to the electorate must not be allowed to obscure the real checks on executive tyranny provided by the evolution first of parliamentary and then of popular democracy.

Although the desire to limit the area of State control was motivated immediately by self-interest, it was nevertheless informed by a more or less coherent political philosophy deriving from Puritan theology. Puritan political philosophy, like Puritan theology, was dominated by a belief in Original Sin and in the Salvation of the Elect. The belief in Original Sin resulted in a distrust both of the competence and of the benevolence of any Government other than a Government of the Saints and in a scepticism towards the possibility of improving man's lot by legislation or by decree. (This did not of course apply to legislation or to decrees relieving Puritans from their political disabilities.) The belief in the Salvation of the Elect led Puritans to regard material prosperity as an outward sign of Salvation and gave them an overweening confidence in the rightness of their own judgment and in the purity of their own intentions. The equation of Salvation with material prosperity, together with the decline of belief in Original Sin and Divine Election led directly to the Utilitarianism into which Nonconformist Puritanism degenerated during the eighteenth century. Utilitarianism was a logical result of Puritanism divorced from its religious content but sustained by the ethical standards derived from its religious origin.

As Puritanism had striven for State toleration in religious matters, so Utilitarianism advocated *laissez faire* in secular matters. The Utilitarian teaching that 'the greatest good of the greatest number' could be achieved by each person following the dictates of his own self-interest derives logically from the Puritan equation of material prosperity with Salvation, once the religious content has been eroded from Puritanism. This teaching, which both justified the apathy of Governments in the face of increasing social injustice, and sanctified the greed of the new industrialists in the midst of their moneymaking, was almost unchallenged at the end of the eighteenth century. By the end of the nineteenth century the application of *laissez faire* principles both in economic and in social matters had become seriously discredited.

In a discussion of the fortunes of *laissez faire* during the nineteenth century one may conveniently equate economic *laissez faire* with the doctrine of Free Trade, and social *laissez faire* with resistance to legislation providing for State social services or for regulating conditions of employment.

After the Napoleonic Wars, an increase in the supply and a fall in the price of imports caused the Government of the day to impose an import duty on corn with the avowed object of supporting the price of home-grown corn in the interest of the agricultural landowners who still dominated Parliament and from whose ranks the Government was almost exclusively recruited. The repeal of the corn duties in 1846 was an indication of the extent to which this domination had passed to the new manufacturing class, to whom cheap bread meant low wages, and whose interest in the matter was thus directly opposed to that of the landowners. During the next half century Free Trade became the symbol of the dominance, the wealth, the self-confidence and the expanding interests of the manufacturing class. It was more than an economic practice, more even than an economic dogma; it was almost a religion. During this half century the radicalism of the Liberal Party, which increased *pari passu* with successive broadenings of the franchise, together with the later identification of the Liberal Party with the policy of Home Rule for Ireland, alienated not only its Whiggish element—its aristocratic supporters—but also the majority of the wealthy middle class who had previously formed its backbone. As a result of this the policy of the Liberal Party tended more and more to reflect the interests of the newly-enfranchised lower-middle and working classes, who were now its principal supporters. At the same time the policy of the Conservative (or Unionist) Party tended more and more to reflect the interests of the wealthy middle class. By the end of the century the enthusiasm of this class for Free

Trade had become considerably modified as a result of growing competition from overseas industrial competitors, particularly from Germany and the United States.

The cult of Free Trade took a long time to die, but the defection of its former high priests not only marked the beginning of the end of Great Britain's commercial and industrial supremacy but also marked the beginning of the end of the political and social dominance of the Puritan middle class, whose self-confidence, independence, and individualism had become indissolubly associated with the economic doctrine of Free Trade. The Protectionist views with which the Unionist Party, now primarily representing the views of manufacturers and big business men, became associated were not a reversion to old mercantile theories but rather an aspect of that collectivism which was beginning to replace individualism in the minds of the masters as well as in the minds of the workers. When the manufacturers started asking for Imperial Preference, tariffs, quotas and so on, and when they started forming Employers' Federations among themselves, they were in effect asking for the same restraints on and safeguards against unrestricted competition as had been demanded on behalf of the factory workers half a century before. Economically the age of individualism and free enterprise was at an end and an age of combination, regulation and 'rationalization' had begun. Socially the qualities which had sustained and sanctioned individualism and free enterprise had outlived their practical usefulness.

Long before this, during the years in which the principles and practices of economic *laissez faire* had become the corner-stone of the British economy, the principles and practices of social *laissez faire* were being steadily eroded. At the beginning of the nineteenth century, fears of the infection of Jacobinism from across the Channel, combined with serious working-class discontent arising from the economic consequences of the Industrial Revolution and the Napoleonic Wars had set in train a process of legislation and a habit of thought, inspired partly by Evangelical philanthropy and partly by fear of revolution, which gradually accepted the principle and practice of State control of conditions of employment and State provision of collective social services in connection with public health, and, later, with education.

It is possible to discern several phases in the relations between the State and the People since the Reformation. First there was the despotic State of the Tudors and early Stuarts when supreme power was vested in the Crown, Then there was a short period when almost equal despotic power was vested in Parliament. Then there were the two Civil Wars followed by a period of experiment under Cromwell. Then, from the Restoration to, approximately, the First Reform Bill there was an oligarchic State in which both Crown and Parliament were controlled by the landed nobility, whose exercise of power was limited both by indolence and by rivalries between themselves (which rivalries were formalized into party warfare between Whigs and Tories). Finally, after 1832, there was the gradual emergence of a democratic State which, broadly speaking, expressed the will of a majority of the people. Up to 1832 resistance to the power of the State was on the one hand a struggle for toleration by the Nonconformists against uniformity, and on the other hand a struggle for power by rising commercial and industrial against traditional landed and clerical interests. After 1832 this struggle gradually took the form of individualist and minority resistance to the encroaching powers of a bureaucratic State. In both periods resistance to the State started as a matter of principle and ended mainly as a matter of self-interest. The principle at issue in the first period was religious, in the second period secular. The interest at issue in the first period was political power and in the second period economic power. In the first period both religious principle and political self-interest prevailed against the power first of the despotic and then of the oligarchic State. In the second period both secular principle and economic self-interest have, on the whole, been in continuous retreat before the encroachments of the State.

During the first half of the nineteenth century the intellectual exponents of *laissez faire* (as distinct from its financial beneficiaries), in whom reason was always stronger than prejudice, and in whom humanitarian sentiments were always stronger than self-interest, found themselves pushed by the logic of events gently but inexorably from a position of resistance to State interference to a position of protest against Parliamentary tolerance of the abuses of *laissez faire*. What had happened was that the Industrial Revolution and the prevailing climate of *laissez faire* had combined to create a situation in which State action was invoked, not to perpetuate oppression, but to succour the oppressed. The Industrial Revolution had forged an economic weapon which gave to its beneficiaries an individual power which outweighed the attenuated political power of the State. Just as in the seventeenth century an individualist assertion had been called for against the despotic power of the State, so in the nineteenth century an assertion of State authority was called for against the despotic power of the individual. And just as in the eighteenth century this individualist assertion led to an attenuation of the authority of the State, so in the twentieth century the assertion of State authority set in train by the abuses of individualism led to an attenuation of the authority of the individual. The clue to the Puritan tradition can be found in its perennial resistance not only to State authority but to the abuse of any authority. Puritanism in authority ceases to be Puritan, because the assumption of authority leads inevitably to those compromises with conscience and with principle which are the antithesis of Puritanism. Puritanism is perennially protestant against the corruptions of power. And when these protests are successful, the protestants themselves become corrupted, bequeathing their protestant mission to a new generation of Puritans. Protest against authority is the first stage in the assumption of authority; resistance to the corruption of power is part of the process of becoming corrupted. The fruits of protest contain the seeds of authority; the fruits of authority contain the seeds of protest.

The achievement of religious toleration and the removal of political disabilities were part of a straightforward process of religious and political protest in which the Puritan role, played by the Nonconformists, was clear and unequivocal. In the struggle for the reassertion of State interference over economic relations between man and man, the role of Puritanism is more uncertain and more confused. Part of the confusion is due to the fact that the development of this interference coincided with the last half century of the struggle for religious toleration and the removal of political and social disabilities. Another cause of confusion was the dual stream in which the Puritan tradition was flowing, with the Utilitarian descendants of the early Puritans in one stream and the Evangelical heirs of Calvinism and Biblical inspiration in the other. The first of these streams approached the social problems of the day with reason tempered by the economic dogmatism of the Benthamites; the second approached them with compassion tempered by the Calvinist tradition of Puritanism and by the aristocratic tradition of Anglicanism. During the first half of the nineteenth century this dual influence was exercised, on the whole, but by no means unanimously and consistently, in favour of State intervention in such matters as public health, relief of destitution, and limitation and regulation of working hours and working conditions. In the second half of the nineteenth century, when the principle of State interference had been more or less established, the Puritan content of the Evangelical tradition tended, in alliance with the Conservative Party, to resist the encroachments of State control, while the Utilitarian tradition became merged, first with Gladstonian Liberalism and then, via the Fabians, who were the intellectual descendants of the Utilitarians, with the rising fortunes of the Labour Party, who advocated not only greatly increased State social services, but also State ownership of the principal means of production.

The continuing influence of the Evangelical revival was social rather than specifically religious. (Its most important religious influence was to provide an unexpected and unintended inspiration for the Oxford Movement.) This social influence, which deeply imbued the English upper and middle classes with the seriousness, sobriety and restraint characteristic of Evangelical laymen like Wilberforce, had a considerable influence on English politics.

During the eighteenth century the venality of English political life was a counterpart of the coarseness and profligacy of the social life of the English governing class. And there was a quality about it even more repellant than its venality—the quality of heartlessness. There was really very little to choose between the political and social morals of the English and of the French aristocracy in the century before the French Revolution. The fact that the English escaped the fate of the French aristocracy is largely due on the one hand to the other-worldly sentiments with which Methodism imbued the masses, and on the other hand to a belated sense of social conscience among the governing class caused, partly it is true by fright, but partly by the influence of Evangelical Christianity. This influence was not so much a specifically religious influence as a social influence which made financial extravagance and ostentation, heartlessness and immorality unfashionable. This new sobriety was influenced not only by the new Puritanism of the Evangelicals but also by the older Puritanism of the middle-class manufacturing magnates (many of whose families had originally been Nonconformists, but had returned to the Establishment with increasing prosperity), like the Peels and the Gladstones, who were beginning to break into the charmed circle of the governing class and who, after 1832, were to dominate it.

In political life, the new sobriety, responsibility and restraint provided very necessary ballast for the ship of State during the troubled years of social upheaval which lasted, roughly, from the end of the Napoleonic Wars to the middle of the century. Although the self-interest of the wealthy remained in the ascendant both in the deliberations of Cabinets and in the legislative activity of Parliaments, the manifestations of self-interest were mitigated by some faint stirrings of conscience, some slight consideration for the human dignity of factory workers and, perhaps more importantly, by a considerable expenditure of mental energy in a not wholly unsuccessful attempt to deal with the new conditions created by new wealth, new cities, new methods of production and a rapidly increasing population.

During those troubled years, slowly, unconsciously and incoherently, the Puritan tradition which had been injected into the governing class both by Evangelical Christianity and by the promotion of the manufacturing magnates, evolved a recognizably Puritan philosophy adapted to the political needs of the time. Material success was still the reward of righteousness but no longer provided its own justification. The belief that material success was the reward of righteousness had to be justified by the use made of material success. True, it could be assumed that the righteousness which made for material success also guaranteed that a right use would be made of material success. But the obligation had to be discharged, not only by acting in such a way as to be a moral example to the unrighteous, but also by acting, if not as a brother, at least as a neighbour towards the unrighteousness and unsuccessful. Receipt of the material rewards of righteousness imposed the obligation of morality in respect of duty towards God and of benevolence in respect of duty towards one's neighbour. In proportion as the sense of duty towards God declined, the sense of duty towards one's neighbour increased. This philosophy, as it broadened out and became consolidated during the second half of the nineteenth century, became the basis of Conservative democracy. The old Utilitarian teaching that the greatest good of the greatest number could be achieved by everyone following the dictates of self-interest was modified into a belief that the greatest good of the greatest number could be achieved as a by-product of the pursuit of self-interest on the part of those who could be trusted to combine self-interest with benevolence and self-restraint. The old Puritan belief in the exemption of the Saved from the limitations imposed by Original Sin was changed into a no less sincere belief in the essential altruism and public-spiritedness of the 'right people'. Rights were conferred by God; duties were expected from those upon whom rights had been so conferred. The idea of a State which conferred rights and exacted duties by legislation was the antithesis of this concept. The State was the channel through which the benevolence of the righteous was exercised and the means by which restraint was conferred on those insufficiently enlightened to practise self-restraint.

This philosophy was evolved alongside with and in opposition to the philosophy of popular power exercised through the

State by means of a Government elected by the people as a whole and operated on behalf of the people as a whole. As against the benevolence and wisdom of the enlightened few this philosophy preached the essential sanctity of the popular will and saw the machinery of State primarily as a means of putting this popular will into effect. In this context the rights of the people were absolute; duties consisted of the submission of the individual inclination to the popular will. To some extent this philosophy represented a return to the role of the medieval State as the arbiter and controller of human behaviour. But with this difference. The medieval State, in intention, claimed to impose the will of God; the modern democratic State claims to impose the will of the people. The Puritan opposition to State control, whether exercised in the name of God or in the name of the people, is based on a dislike and distrust of collectivism in whatever name it claims to be operating. With the early Puritans, pursuit of self-interest derived from an individualist philosophy; with their nineteenth-century descendants, an individualist philosophy derived from the pursuit of self-interest.

In an age when the franchise was being gradually extended until it became almost universal, individualism, as a practical political philosophy, had to produce fruits both of efficiency and of benevolence in order to compete effectively with collectivism. In practice, and in so far as modern democratic politics are informed by any principle at all, Conservative philosophy is individualist within the framework of collectivism imposed by the spirit of the time.

The notes of this individualism are characteristic of secular Puritanism. There is an ingrained belief in the connection between poverty and idleness and a consequent exaltation of the virtues of hard work. There is a conviction of the necessity for individual thrift, both as the basis for investment and, in the form of insurance, as the basis for State welfare schemes. That is to say, both investment and welfare should be financed out of the voluntary saving derived from individual thrift and not out of the compulsorily levied proceeds of State taxation. For the same reason there is the profound feeling that all services, medical, educational and so on, sought and paid for individually, are essentially superior to similar services provided by the State.

These notes provided much of the impetus behind England's economic expansion during the nineteenth century. But the energy and self-reliance which they implied were not accompanied by as much benevolence as was needed to justify them to the expanding electorate. This resulted in an acceleration of the swing-back from *laissez faire* to State control until a stage was reached when the community, acting through the machinery of the State, having assumed most of the social duties, not unnaturally denied the rights of the self-appointed Elect. The failure of individualism was essentially a failure of benevolence. The concept of social duty as a justification for the pursuit of self-interest was evolved too late, and partook too much of the nature of an after-thought.

Among the Victorian governing class, the duty of benevolence was at war with the instinct for accumulation. The economic and social climate in which they lived weighed the scales heavily in favour of accumulation. People lived frugally, not in order to give of their superfluity, but in order to re-invest it. Consequently, in modern Conservatism, individualism has been tempered, not by voluntary benevolence, but by the compulsory redistributive machinery of the Welfare State which Conservatism has been reluctantly compelled to sponsor as a condition of survival.

In a twentieth-century democracy operating under conditions of universal suffrage, a political Party which openly advocated and acted upon a belief in the pursuit of individual self-interest tempered by benevolence as a motivating principle in the conduct of the State would be condemned to perpetual opposition. Benevolent autocracy is no more practicable in the England of to-day than the Rule of the Saints was in the England of the seventeenth century. Thus the principle of individualism, which insists on the rights and accepts the consequent duties of the individual (as distinct from a mere smash-and-grab individualism actuated by no principle at all), is a minority movement even within the Party most sympathetic to it. Its influence as a minority movement is limited by its almost complete divorce from the

Christian belief which is the only logical justification for individualism. (The claim of the individual to assert himself against
the community is derived from the peculiar dignity conferred
on the individual by God in the Incarnation. An individualist
ant is almost a grotesque conception; but the essential difference
between a man and an ant is that God became Incarnate not in
an ant but in a man.) Within this limitation, individualism does
keep alive the human virtues of self-reliance, self-control, sober
living, hard work and voluntary benevolence, even though it
has forgotten the essential reason for doing so. If and when it
rediscovers this essential reason, individualism will come to be
equated less with self-interest and more with human dignity.
Its protest against the encroachments of collectivism will then
become more effective than it is to-day.

The most characteristic Puritan politician of the nineteenth
century was the Earl of Shaftesbury. An aristocrat by birth and
by temperament, an ascetic by nature and a fervent Evangelical
by conviction, he disliked and distrusted democracy and believed
in achieving reforms not by the political enfranchisement and
education of the masses but by the benevolence and personal
service of the privileged classes. It is ironical that, as a result of the
reforms which, by his sincerity and his energy, he imposed on a
reluctant Parliament, he created a fashion for State interference
and helped to lay the foundations of a Welfare State which he
would have detested. In his old age he bitterly opposed the
Education Bill of 1870 which was seen by many as a logical
development of the reforms which he sponsored in his earlier
life. He found himself almost equally at variance with the Christian
Socialists, who wished to imbue the democracy of the masses
with the Christian principles in which he himself believed, and
with the agnostic benevolence of the school of Charles Dickens.
His political attitude was informed entirely by his religious
beliefs, which the march of science had rendered unfashionable
and, in some sort, ridiculous. The political isolation in which he
spent his old age is indicative of the extent to which the political
Puritanism of which he is the outstanding nineteenth-century
representative, was dependent on its religious content. In him

consciousness of privilege was fructified by a sense of duty; his Puritan tendency to self-righteousness was chastened by Christian humility; his natural sympathies were heightened by Christian compassion and limited by a belief in Original Sin which caused him to fear the results of almost any activity directed by anyone not of like mind with himself. He had no political successor of any importance. The individualist tradition which he inherited and enriched was later sustained by self-interest and limited by an instinct for self-preservation. Dislike of democracy was dictated not by a belief in Original Sin but by a distaste for any wide distribution of the fruits of privilege and power. Sobriety of life was enjoined, not by the habit of asceticism, but by the urge for material accumulation. Righteousness was practised in the hope of reward, not in the next world, but in this.

Nevertheless men like Shaftesbury, and Wilberforce before him, set an enduring fashion in respectability which no politician could afford to neglect. Public men had to assume a virtue even if they had it not. They had to pay lip service to ideas and to ideals which many of them privately derided. And lip service paid in the temple of democracy is apt to impose specific performance on the part of those who have uttered it. And so, if the substance of that in which Wilberforce and Shaftesbury believed perished with them, the shadow thereof remained to soften the harsh light of Victorian governing class acquisitiveness and to tone down the consequent bitterness of antagonism between class and class, until much of that which they had hoped to achieve by compassion expressed in personal service was at length in some sort achieved by the democratic processes which they had unwittingly encouraged and which they vehemently abhorred.

CHAPTER V

The Puritan Tradition in Social Life

IT is convenient to consider the Puritan social characteristics of hard work and sober living together with the economic virtues of enterprise and capital accumulation which flowed from them. In other lands and in other ages—in Renaissance Italy for example—the fruits of hard work and enterprise had been spent in the creation of a civilization. In England the fruits of hard work and enterprise were husbanded for the creation of an economic system appropriate to the efficient exploitation of those material opportunities which geographical discoveries and technical inventions were calling into being. The aristocracy which the Tudors had raised from the plundered riches of the medieval Church were interested not so much in capital accumulation and investment as in the use of their privileges to maintain and if possible to increase their high rate of income for the purpose of lavish spending. For them money was primarily a means of living and of spending lavishly. Puritan application and energy, given the opportunities of the times, inevitably brought wealth to the ablest of them. Their religious beliefs and their social habits made lavish spending unattractive to them, and the same application and energy, and the same opportunities, which had enabled them to make money in the first place, pointed the way to its further use in speculation, in investment and in expansion.

In the sixteenth and seventeenth centuries capital accumulation was achieved, to a much greater extent than is the case to-day, as the result of individual acts of conscious restraint from spending in accordance with the definition of the classical economists. This conscious restraint was encouraged and, as it were, sanctified by a mystique which was derived from religious Puritanism and which provided the principal driving force behind England's economic expansion. The basis of this mystique was the belief that material prosperity was an outward and visible sign of Divine approval. The prevalence of this belief may be attributed partly to the influence of the 'success stories' of the Old Testament, and partly to the fact that the Puritan's renunciation of sensual pleasure forced him to find emotional compensation in the satisfactions of material success. The Puritan did not abandon the world; he only abandoned half of it, with the result that his energies and desires became concentrated on the other half.

Insensibly, the original sequence by which sobriety and diligence were the fruits of Salvation and riches the result of sobriety and diligence became reversed. In practice, sober living and religious observance came to be regarded as the fruit and not as the cause of material prosperity, as the ornaments and not as the conditions of success. Conversely, poverty came to be regarded as disgraceful in itself and licentious behaviour and irreligion merely as incidental and regrettable results of poverty. Thus was evolved a puritanical aristocracy of material wealth, restricted not by heredity but by Predestination and distinguished, not by lavish expenditure and licentious behaviour, but by prudence and sobriety. In this aristocracy, religion became almost as much a matter of conventional observance and almost as little an influence on life as it was led, as did the religion of the landed aristocracy. The objective of religious toleration became not a spiritual desire for liberty of conscience but a material desire to be relieved of social and political disability. The objective of political liberty became, or rather remained (for the Puritan tradition had never been democratic), a determination to secure inclusion in the closed ring of political privilege and power.

The notes of this new aristocracy played a decisive part in the shaping of post-Reformation England. The habit of sober living conserved and concentrated energy on the one hand and provided for capital accumulation on the other. The identification of poverty with idleness on the one hand and with the Will of God on the other blunted the social conscience and brought England to the verge of a revolution from which she was only saved by another and more compassionate spiritual awakening. The emphasis on the accumulation rather than the spending of wealth, while it provided the capital for the new machines and for the new enterprises that were to make England rich, led to a grave impoverishment of all those arts which previously had depended on the patronage and on the good taste of moneyed men.

The relevance of this social philosophy to the needs of an expanding economy and to the ambitions of a rising class of manufacturers and merchants ensured that its outward manifestations spread both upwards and downwards through the whole of the increasingly important and increasingly numerous middle class. But both upper and lower classes remained almost untouched by this sobriety until Methodism influenced the lower class in the direction of self-respect and the Evangelical Revival influenced the upper class in the direction of respect for others. But in the up-and-coming middle class there were obvious attractions in a religion and in a social outlook which sanctified men's ambition, justified their selfishness, and castigated the vices which they had neither the time nor the inclination to pursue.

This middle-class England, by virtue of the wealth, the energy, the enfranchisement and the education which its Puritan ancestry had enabled it to acquire, set the tone of English life during the Victorian era and consequently stamped that era both with its social virtues and with its social vices.

The apogee of the propertied middle class may be said to lie between the passing of the first Reform Bill in 1832 and the passing of the second Reform Bill in 1878. The first Reform Bill brought political power to this class; the second Reform Bill started the process, completed in 1928, by which political power ceased to be the monopoly of the few and became vested in the people as a whole (a doctrine which was held by the Levellers and vigorously repelled and repressed by the Puritan Independents).

The social morality of nineteenth-century Puritanism was derived both from its religious origins and from a purely secular belief in money as being the ultimate regulator of all human relationships. Just as Reservation of the Sacrament leads inevitably to Adoration, so it seems that the accumulation of money leads no less inevitably to its being endowed with an ethical significance.

The basis of sacramental religion is the belief that the Grace of God sanctifies and completes nature—that nature is sanctified and completed by being offered to God and by being received back from God imbued with the Holy Spirit of God. The Puritan saw the Grace of God as overcoming and driving out nature. To live by Grace was the Puritan alternative to living by nature. The mark of the good life was the extent to which nature was subdued by Grace. What happened in practice was that the simpler and more obvious manifestations of nature were subjugated and replaced by more complicated and more recondite manifestations which were mistaken for signs of Grace. In this way covetousness, domestic tyranny and uncharitableness of all kinds were not only unrecognized as vices, but cherished as virtues.

It is easy to paint too black a picture of the gloom and misery shed by this systematic attempt to subordinate instead of to sanctify the impulses of human nature. The manifestations of belief in the essential goodness of human nature lead to at least as much misery as the manifestations of belief in its essential vileness. The 'pleasant vices' are not always so very pleasant, and the fruits of licence are apt to be no less ugly than the fruits of repression. Bullying legitimate children is less of an evil than abandoning illegitimate ones; preoccupation with gathering the fruits of one's own labour is less reprehensible than a determination to live off the fruits of other people's. Enforcement of hypocritical piety is better than encouragement of lawless debauchery. One cannot rightly appraise the excesses of nineteenth-century Puritanism without appreciating the extent to which these excesses were a reaction from and a protest against the immorality and laxity of nearly all classes of society during the eighteenth century, and without appreciating the dangers of revolution and chaos into which this immorality and laxity had so nearly led England. The sheer brutality of that eighteenth-century life which seethed beneath the thin crust of aristocratic refinement and moderation and *bon ton* presents an appearance of rude vitality and causes us sometimes to ignore its essential degradation. The Puritan prescription of Strength through Misery was perhaps a salutary antidote to the cult of Weakness through Joy.

But the cult of misery in this world as the condition of escape from hell-fire in the next was the somewhat incoherent framework of a more or less exact pattern of human relationships based on the cash nexus. This aspect of Puritan morality is more important, because more enduring, than the theological aspect.

According to this morality, financial independence was the essential condition of liberty, and the essential basis of charity. The possession of money was desiderated, and the pursuit of it made respectable, because it endowed the possessor with liberty and gave him the opportunity for benevolence. Conversely, lack of money deprived a man not only of the enjoyment of, but also the right to, liberty, and degraded him from the dignity of dispensing, to the humiliation of receiving, charity. Financial independence conferred rights; financial dependence imposed duties. The rights of a parent over a child, an employer over an employee, a patron over an object of charity, were conferred by the financial dependence of the one on the other. A father ceased to have any rights over his son as soon as the son was financially independent; if in his old age the father became financially dependent on the son, it was the father's duty to submit himself to the son's wishes. Much of the energy and driving force of the Victorian middle class was derived from the feeling of servility which was associated with financial dependence. This attitude of mind meant that the whole subject of money and property became hedged about with a peculiar sanctity. Great store was laid on the inviolability of a financial contract. Business failure or bankruptcy was regarded as a disgrace rather than as a misfortune; a man losing his money was the equivalent of a woman losing her virtue. In either case extenuating circumstances of Act of God or of rape merely meant that the unfortunate one became an object of charity rather than of obloquy.

This sanctification of property conditioned the characteristic Puritan attitude towards sex. Middle-class women were, in the nineteenth century, with rare exceptions, financially dependent upon men—upon their fathers before, and upon their husbands after, marriage. A man who enjoyed a woman's body without financially supporting her was stealing something from the man who did financially support her. For a married woman to commit adultery or for an unmarried girl to give herself to a lover while being financially supported by her father was a crime against property. It was not a case of discrimination against women as such. The male seducer was essentially guilty of the same crime against property. The woman had, so to speak, abstracted, and the man had received, the stolen goods. But for a man to consort with a prostitute or to keep a mistress was less heinous because no crime against property was involved.

There was a more creditable side to the Puritan attitude in matters of sex. Begetting an illegitimate child was equivalent to incurring a debt which one was unable to pay. The fulfilment of a material obligation was an essential moral duty. Failure to fulfil a material obligation was the essence of immorality. The performance of an action likely to lead to incurring a material obligation which one was unable to fulfil made that action immoral. Practically the only way in which a man could be sure of fulfilling his obligations towards a child begotten by him was to be both married and solvent.

It would be wrong to say that the nineteenth-century Puritan did not recognize a moral as well as a material obligation. But a moral obligation was only valid if it could be expressed in material terms. Puritan ethics consisted of moral obligations translated into material terms.

This intense sense of personal obligations owed and due made the nineteenth-century Puritan extremely suspicious of any State interference in relationships between man and man. He was quite unable to distinguish morally between charity dispensed by private benevolence and between social services dispensed by the State from the proceeds of taxation, except that the recipients of the latter were even more degraded than the recipients of the former because they felt themselves relieved from the duty of gratitude towards their benefactors, and except that the benefactors themselves were unable to derive the same feeling of virtue from the payment of a compulsory tax as they were from the donation of a voluntary subscription. To receive benefits from another instead of earning the means to pay for them oneself was regarded as a degradation resulting from idleness; to endow the recipient with such benefits as of right, instead of compelling him to repay them with gratitude and servility, was seen as an encouragement of idleness.

This distrust of idleness was combined with a contempt for what are regarded as harmless amusements, and with an exaggerated Sabbatarianism. All these were characteristics of the early Puritans, and it is necessary to trace the habits of thought which fixed these beliefs and prejudices so firmly in the Puritan mind.

Even after the original religious impulse had weakened, the Puritan mind was still dominated by a conviction of Original Sin. But the conviction of personal Salvation had weakened with the weakening of the religious impulse, and this led to alternating moods of self-assertion and self-distrust. 'Satan finds mischief for idle hands.' This was a favourite saying among nineteenth-century Puritans. Although it was openly applied to others, it was secretly attributed to themselves. The financial urge in favour of accumulation and against extravagance was reinforced by a moral aversion both to idleness itself and to the means employed for beguiling idleness. They had continually to reassure themselves of Salvation by a continual reassertion of their rejection of the allurements of the flesh and by a continual re-emphasis of their sense of responsibility. Just as many modern American business men develop a neurosis derived from fear of failure in this world and influenced by twenty-five year-old memories of the Great Slump, so many Victorian business men developed a neurosis derived from fear of damnation in the next world and influenced by childhood stories about hell-fire. The Victorian neurosis took the form of a morbid intensity of application and a morbid rejection of relaxation. The American neurosis takes the form of a morbid determination to relax combined with a constitutional inability to do so.

Sabbatarianism was an aspect of this morbid dread of idleness.

In all religions the importance attached to a particular abstinence is proportional to the importance attached to the corresponding indulgence. This does not apply only to carnal indulgences. The importance attached by the Puritan to earning his living heightened the importance which he attached to observance of the Fourth Commandment. But it was important to ensure that this enforced idleness did not imperil Salvation by leading to the indulgence which idleness encouraged and with which idleness was beguiled. Such indulgences, sinful in any event, would be infinitely more sinful on the occasion of what was, so to speak, a divinely appointed and (to use a word which the Puritan would have indignantly rejected) ritual idleness. Hence the almost legendary, and certainly exaggerated, terrors of the Puritan Victorian Sunday.

These Puritan abstinences and severities were only practised in their full rigour by a comparatively small number of people. But the habit of mind which motivated them had a deep influence on social life, and particularly on middle-class social life, during the Victorian era. So much so that in popular parlance the word Victorian is synonymous with the Puritan characteristics we have described. In our own day, social habits and, to a much greater extent, social laws are deeply coloured by the practices and beliefs of nineteenth-century Puritanism. The fact that there is, on Sundays in England, no horse racing, no professional cricket or football, and very few other organized amusements, is an obvious residue of nineteenth-century Puritanism in a society which is gradually abandoning the habit of regarding Sunday as a holy day. The divorce laws which, congruent neither with Christian nor with civil ideas of marriage, regard divorce as a punishment awarded for adultery or desertion, are relics of the Puritan conception of human relationships. The Puritan equation of State aid with charity in such matters as the National Health Service, the Old Age Pension and State education, is not entirely dead among a section of the middle class. For many people poverty, and in particular the receipt of Public Assistance, is a disgrace rather than a misfortune. The equation of financial independence with liberty and poverty with idleness still colours much middle-class thinking. It is not fashionable to say in public that a man in receipt of Public Assistance has no right to vote; but such a view is still commonly held in private in middle-class circles, and such a view certainly remains dominant in middle-class family relationships.

The idea that anyone has a natural right to anything implies a moral egalitarianism which is abhorrent to the Puritan. Charles I's head was still on his shoulders when Independents and Levellers started quarrelling about this fundamental point of inherent human rights. Orthodox Puritan ideas about liberty did not include any belief in inherent human rights. Rights, like everything else, had to be earned. This later degenerated into the view that rights, like everything else, had to be bought.

This reduction of human obligations and human rights to a cash basis was not so very different from some of the abuses of the medieval Church. But, to the Puritan, money was merely the measure of human rights and obligations. The purchase of rights still imposed obligations which had to be discharged in other than financial terms. And, unlike the medieval Christian, the Puritan, burdened and dignified with the habit and duty of individual judgment, was always more than half-conscious of the extent to which he had compromised his religion to suit his self-interest. Such half-consciousness, which was at the roots of his doubts of his own Salvation, is perhaps the key to the strains and stresses which racked the Puritan soul.

The most serious social deficiency of Puritanism was in the quality of its human relationships. There was no social content in the Puritan religion; it was a solitary affair between the individual and his Maker; there was no Sacramental content to sanctify social institutions or to consecrate human relationships. The barriers which the Puritan saw as having been removed between himself and God were set up instead between God and all the manifestations of nature. The Puritan, in his approach to God, endeavoured to leave his human nature behind him and so, by his deliberate act, human nature and all human relationships remained unsanctified.

Relations between man and man were seen as being on an

inferior plane to relations between man and God, and not as an inseparable part of relations between man and God. Love of man for man was regarded as being almost the antithesis instead of being the essential complement of the love of man for God. To love man as a result of loving God is almost as difficult as it is to love man as a preliminary to loving God. The only way is to learn to love God and man simultaneously as a result of learning to love Christ who is both God and Man. The Puritans never really learnt this. They loved Christ as the Son of God but not as the Son of Man. Their habit of trying to dissociate their human nature from their approaches to God inevitably degraded their attitude towards human relationships. They did not see that their approach to other people was an inseparable part of their approach to God. Their attitude towards other people was regulated not by love but by a sense of duty. They were just but they were not always merciful. They paid their debts but they did not always forgive their debtors. They believed that God's Kingdom was not of this world, but they sometimes forgot that this world is a part of God's Kingdom. Believing themselves to be the Elect of God's Kingdom, they tended to look on the world as a foreign country, as a place where they had been sent to work, and as a testing-ground for their suitability to be numbered among the Elect. This baffling mixture of worldliness and other-worldliness may be likened to the attitude of a European in a heathen land, who is intent on making a fortune with which to establish his position in the land from which he came and to which he hopes to return. He has to set a good example to the heathen; he has punctually to fulfil any obligations entered into with them; and he has if possible to live at peace with them. He has even to use the language of brotherhood towards them; but in his attitude there is nothing of sympathy, nothing of understanding and no sense of any common purpose extending beyond the day-to-day transactions of this life.

Puritan individualism was to a large extent a refusal to become over-involved with the affairs of a community with which he was unable wholly to identify himself. The Puritan was only prepared to involve himself to the extent that was necessary both to safeguard his own interests and to fulfil and to exact the material and moral obligations which he rated so highly.

The result was a way of life deficient in sympathy but great with responsibility; lacking in compassion but regulated with justice; fruitful in good works but arid in comradeship; well-furnished with material things but singularly lacking in beauty and grace; dependent, for all its godliness, upon material profusion and lacking in resources to compensate for material ill-fortune. Diligence, sobriety and obedience were the principal virtues; idleness, extravagance and rebellion the principal vices.

A society consisting entirely of Puritans would have been intolerable; a man possessing all the characteristics of the Puritan is somewhat forbidding. But a measure of Puritanism is a valuable ingredient both in society and in the individual character.

Unregenerate man being what he is, and unregenerate human society being what it is, the element of Puritanism which has become woven into the English character is valuable both as a brake on irresponsibility and as a spur to indolence. Too much Puritanism dehumanizes human relationships; too little Puritanism results in their being all too human. Those who believe in the fundamental goodness of human nature will have little good to say of Puritanism; those who accept the validity of the doctrine of Original Sin, whether as a result of Christian belief or of dispassionate observation, will recognize in Puritanism a salutary prophylactic against man's natural tendency to degeneration. It would be an exaggeration to say that Puritanism represents the national and the individual conscience; Puritanism has too many blind spots for that. Puritanism may more truly be given the role of the national and the individual hair-shirt.

Whether the expanding national economy evoked the virtues and vices of Puritanism, or whether Puritanism was a fortunate and fortuitous contemporary circumstance which enabled existing economic circumstances to be efficiently exploited is a matter for endless and not very profitable debate. What probably happened was that Puritanism both influenced and was influenced by the national economy. In its application to the national economy Puritanism was a source of strength both in its worldly and in its other-worldly aspects. Worldliness tends to be satisfied with and to try to conserve things as they are; other-worldliness is apt to be insufficiently interested in material things either to attempt to conserve or to improve them. Puritanism got the best of both worlds. The aspect of worldliness in Puritanism ensured an interest in material things; the aspect of other-worldliness ensured an indifference to comfort and to custom which resisted the worldly temptations to conservatism and to complacency.

The vast accumulation of wealth which took place in England during the nineteenth century would not have been possible in a society which greatly enjoyed spending the proceeds of wealth. The abstinence and hard work involved would not have been possible except in a society which neutralized the natural human tendency to dissipation and idleness by making a religion of their opposites. The necessary toughness of fibre would not have been achieved except in a society which almost came to regard failure as equivalent to moral delinquency.

The Puritan is a revolutionary in that he has no innate reverence for things as they are; he is a conservative in that he has a great reverence for property. He believes in liberty in that he objects to the State assuming more than a minimum of authority over the individual; he objects to democracy in that he objects to the individual being subjected to the interests and opinions of a majority. His belief in liberty, in effect, excludes belief in democracy.

This corpus of Puritan beliefs and qualities constituted the political and social morality of Victorian middle-class England, and as such constituted the dominant English way of life during the middle years of the nineteenth century. Both the aristocracy and the working class were influenced by it, but they did not wholly absorb it. The aristocracy, which gradually became little more than the upper crust of the middle class, tended to grow out of it. The working class, in a political democracy advancing steadily towards universal adult suffrage, on the one hand equated State control with the advancement of their own interests, and on the other hand, having improved their lot, not by individualism but by combination, had little respect for those moral virtues which derived from individualism.

A morality which ceases to be able to impose itself on society as a whole gradually loses its hold upon the class from which that morality is derived. Economic individualism was both sustained and justified by Puritan morality, just as Puritan morality was sustained and justified by the fruits of economic individualism. As economic individualism receded before collectivism (in the form both of State control and of commercial monopoly and 'rationalisation') so the habit of Puritan morality, which no longer bore its previous material fruits and no longer enjoyed its consequent social prestige, became discredited. Restraints which were no longer sanctified by being associated with material success became stigmatized as repressions. Economies which no longer fructified as fortunes became regarded as meannesses. Disciplines which became ends in themselves instead of means to self-enrichment became considered as oppressions. Outward piety, when no longer associated with great possessions, became denounced as hypocrisy. Weaknesses which appear as the concomitants of success are almost regarded as virtues; virtues which are, perforce, their own reward are almost regarded as weaknesses. The gradual change in economic climate has tended to make the austerities of Puritanism ridiculous and, as a natural consequence, has made the practice of these austerities considerably less popular.

To what extent is Puritan morality an infliction justified by its economic virtues, and to what extent has it a continuing validity in our national life apart from its economic context? It is only theoretically a question as to whether the Puritan way of life is superior to any other way of life. The practical question is whether such remnant of Puritanism as exists in English social life to-day tends to improve that life or to deprave it. Is it a valuable part of our heritage or is it a tiresome anachronism?

Puritanism, in its modern context, has become almost completely divorced from its original religious inspiration. Such specifically religious belief as there is in England to-day—which, broadly speaking, is either sacramental or revivalist, owes little or nothing to the Puritan tradition. But the Puritan tradition does have a salutary effect on secular morality in that it continues to insist and to act upon a belief in the implications of Original Sin or, to use a secular term, of natural depravity. Presumably because Original Sin has a specifically Christian connotation, and because of the influence bequeathed by such men as Rousseau, Locke, Darwin, and, latterly, by Freud and the school of pseudo-scientific Viennese psycho-analytical charlatans, Western secular morality is heavily biassed in favour of natural virtue. To this the Puritan tradition, from which the Christian element has been sufficiently eroded as to make it acceptable to secular prejudices, supplies some corrective.

Belief in Original Sin is the key to Puritan morality. The secularization of Puritanism did not destroy this belief; it merely translated it into secular terms. Redemption from Original Sin by Salvation was secularized into terms of a permanent battle against depravity by applying vigilance to oneself and restraint to others.

The morality which believes in liberating natural virtue by allowing free play to the natural impulses and believes that people will behave properly if, by fair treatment, decent living conditions and so on, they are given the chance to do so, is the antithesis of Puritanism. It is also the antithesis of Christian belief. The significance of the Puritan tradition in this connection is that it does provide some corrective to the results of this morality in circles which are quite impervious to Christian teaching.

It is a matter of observation that material and moral incentives and/or material and moral restraints are necessary to ensure a tolerable standard of behaviour in any human society. In the economic and social climate of to-day the Puritan tradition is more obviously operative in the restraints which it imposes than in the incentives which it provides. In a peaceful England, when extravagance is good for trade and when pleasure is regarded almost as a biological necessity, the restraints associated with Puritanism are necessarily unpopular. In an England at war, when extravagance and pleasure are unpatriotic and when the capacity to endure is a condition of survival, the austerities associated with Puritanism assume a certain grandeur.

Society as a whole has been unable to comprehend the Christian ideal of sanctifying nature. Instead it has alternated between acting as if nature were fundamentally good and acting as if nature were irredeemably evil. Excessive manifestations of the one concept have been corrected by the reaction caused by these excesses in favour of the other concept. In this context Puritanism is representative of the view that nature is irredeemably evil. The prevalence of this view, and the excesses deriving from this prevalence, caused an automatic reaction in favour of the other view, the excesses of which generate an almost automatic Puritan corrective. These opposing views are inextricably woven into the fabric of English society, as they are inextricably woven into the character of most English individuals. This may be said to give to English society and to many English individuals an element of hypocrisy and an element of neurosis. It may also be said to give to both an element of balance. This balance provides that no social theories, no individual prejudices, are carried to their logical conclusions. Paradoxically Puritanism, with its distrust of compromise, has done much to endow the English character with its taste for compromise. For, when the implications of natural virtue become intolerable, the Englishman turns empirically to Puritanism; when the implications of Puritanism become intolerable he empirically and temporarily adopts the thesis of natural virtue. The Puritan tradition provides that reactions from the thesis of natural virtue take a specifically Puritan colour. Puritanism is the medicine by which excesses of self-mistrust, derived from a mistaken reliance on the resources of natural virtue, are converted, first into self-confidence, then into complacency, and finally into a nemesis of self-assertion.

CHAPTER VI

The Puritan Tradition and Liberty

THE purpose of this chapter is to examine such contributions as were made by Puritanism to the theory and practice of political and intellectual liberty in England.

As we have seen, a characteristic note of Puritanism was rejection of the religious authority of the Church and, by derivation from that, rejection of the absolute authority of the Crown claimed by the doctrine of the Divine Right of Kings. Supreme authority, according to orthodox Puritan theory, resided only in God, and interpretation of that authority was a matter for the judgment of the individual as applied to Holy Scripture, regarded as the authentic Word of God.

To what extent was this view of religious authority reflected in Puritan views about the liberty of the individual? To what extent, if at all, can the Independent Puritans be regarded as advocating those principles of individual liberty which are regarded as axiomatic in England to-day? Was the Independents' insistence on the right of congregations to elect and to dismiss their own Ministers the religious counterpart of the secular ideals of liberty and democracy which were later to find expression in *Habeas Corpus*, popular and legal recognition of the rights of minorities, and, ultimately, in universal suffrage?

In order to answer these questions it is necessary to consider the limitations placed by Puritan religious beliefs on the liberty of worship which they claimed for religious congregations. These limitations were both implicit and explicit. Implicitly, liberty of worship was claimed not for all men in accordance with some supposed natural right, but only for those elected to Salvation and consequently held to possess the facility of knowing the Will of God. Explicitly the Independents denied any freedom of worship on the one hand to those who believed in Episcopacy

87

and on the other hand to those who denied the Doctrine of the Trinity. In brief, they advocated religious liberty only in so far as the results of that liberty were likely to be in accordance with their own views. They believed in the liberty of people like themselves to do what they liked in religious matters. Their attitude towards liberty in secular affairs was subject to similar limitations. They were prepared neither to concede political liberty to their political opponents not to grant political power to their social inferiors.

Belief in liberty is incompatible with a belief in the infallibility of one's own convictions, since a belief in liberty implies a conscious readiness to acknowledge the possibility that one's own convictions do not possess universal validity. The Independent Puritans did not possess any such scepticism about their convictions. Cromwell once implored the Rump 'in the bowels of Christ' to consider the possibility that they might be mistaken. But such a possibility very rarely occurred either to Cromwell himself or to the Independent Puritans, possibly because they were not accustomed to thinking in terms of Christ's Compassion. A Calvinist belief was not really compatible with belief in the possibility of being mistaken in fundamental matters, since belief in the possibility of being so mistaken implied belief in the possibility of eternal damnation.

Just as the orthodox Puritan rejected the thesis of a natural authority inherent in the people, so he rejected the thesis of natural liberties belonging to the people. He was more concerned with the nature of authority than the way in which authority was used. A rightly constituted authority—that is to say an authority approved by the individual judgment of the Elect—was not circumscribed in the use of that authority by any necessity to concede certain 'natural' liberties. Conversely, a wrongly constituted authority could not commend itself to the Elect by the concession of such 'natural' liberties.

The Calvinist beliefs of the orthodox Puritan inhibited any belief in natural liberty. Calvinism is essentially an aristocratic and authoritarian creed. In Calvinist belief the potential absolute authority of a ruler is limited neither by law, nor by the existence

of any 'natural' rights or contracts, but by the lack of any hierarchic system for the transmission and acceptance of that authority.
Such civil liberties as orthodox Puritanism achieved were the
result, not of any libertarian principles, but a by-product of the
destruction of traditional and hierarchic authority. The rejection
of Calvinism was a necessary preliminary to the development of
libertarian principles. The fact that such principles did gain some
currency (although no official acceptance) during the Puritan
Revolution is due to the fact that Calvinist beliefs were rejected
by a considerable body of Puritans.

The Puritan Revolution moved steadily to the left until it was
checked in mid-career by Cromwell. First the Presbyterian
majority in the Long Parliament transferred to themselves the
authority previously vested in the Crown. Then the Independent
majority in the Army usurped the authority of the Long Parliament by purging it of its Presbyterian majority. At this point
Cromwell and Ireton intervened to prevent a further leftward
movement towards the Leveller principles which were strongly
represented in the Army. This leftward movement, if pursued,
would have led to the effective assumption of authority by the
people as a whole. The point at which the Revolution was
halted was not therefore an arbitrary one. The point at
which Independents and Levellers parted company was the point
of departure between the implications of Calvinism and the
implications of a belief in natural rights. The Calvinists believed
in Divine Authority exercised through the Rule of the Saints—
that is to say through the rule of those who had been endowed
with a knowledge of God's Purpose by Divine Election. This
excluded a belief in inherent rights or in fundamental liberties.
The Levellers implicitly, and sometimes explicitly, abandoned
Calvinism and all but abandoned any belief in effective Divine
Authority. Instead they believed in the People as the ultimate
source of authority. Any existing authority was held by implied
mandate from the People, and was replaceable at the will of
the People. At the same time, and with varying degrees of emphasis, they believed in the inviolability of certain fundamental
liberties which they apparently believed would be automatically

G   89

safe-guarded by the effective exercise of popular authority. The Independents and the Levellers both believed in the desirability of certain liberties—liberty of worship (within limits in the case of the Independents), freedom from arbitrary arrest and imprisonment and so on. But there were two fundamental points of difference. Whereas the Independents were prepared to give a limited application to such liberties as part of an immediate political programme, the Levellers believed in their universal application as a fundamental human right to be written into the law of the land. And whereas the Levellers assumed that democracy would constitute a guarantee for the preservation of these liberties, the Independents realized, as the Levellers did not, the tyrannical possibilities of democracy. The Levellers sought to reconcile the preservation of liberty with the practice of democracy by insisting on the observance of ancient laws and customs which, according to them, had been ignored by previous rulers. The Independents, who believed that the Divine Will as interpreted by themselves superseded any laws and customs, ancient or modern, would have none of this. When the Independents protested against tyranny they based their protest on the ungodliness of the tyrant. When the Levellers protested against tyranny they protested against the illegality of the tyrant. But their protests were founded, not on specific laws, but on the natural law which they regarded as underlying all laws. Since this natural law was inseparable from the natural right from which the authority of the people was derived, it followed that the exercise of this natural right could not conflict with obedience to the natural law.

John Milton, in his writings, occupied a position midway between the Independents and the Levellers. He believed in natural law and in the liberties attaching to it, but he did not believe that observance of natural law was likely to come about as a result of the sovereignty of the people. He believed in an aristocracy of wise men who would rule by the light of their wisdom and in accordance with natural law.

There is a general tendency to believe in the innate capacity of one's own kind to govern. Theories about authority tend to be conditioned by the status of the men advancing these theories. Men start advancing theories to justify their assumption of power when the prospect of power appears to be within their reach. The Leveller doctrine of the sovereignty of the people was not so much a philosophic idea as a realization of the fact that the ferment set in train by the execution of Strafford and Laud, by the Civil War and by the victories of the Model Army had reached a point at which the common soldiers of the New Model were within measurable distance of attaining power. The fact that they did not attain power was due to the fact that the Independents' idea of the Army as an instrument of God proved stronger and more acceptable to the Army as a whole than the Leveller idea of the Army as the representatives of the people.

Similarly the idea of liberty is apt to be conditioned by the particular forms of liberty which happen to be important to and valued by the kind of men who are advancing the idea of liberty. The real difference between a libertarian and an authoritarian is that a libertarian is prepared to accord to others those liberties which he happens to value for himself and those which, when applied to others, do not impose restrictions on himself. By this token, Milton had libertarian ideas about divorce and the censorship, but about very little else.

There is nothing specifically Puritan about the democratic and libertarian ideas which gained currency as a result of the ferment set up by the Puritan Revolution. They were in fact the antithesis of Puritanism in that they set up the ideal of the self-interest of the majority against the Puritan ideal of the God-guided conscience of the minority. Such factors as the personality of Cromwell, the prestige of property and the social and religious atmosphere of the time ensured the immediate defeat of Leveller ideas. But the essential doctrine of the Levellers, secularized and purged of cant in the Benthamite concept of the greatest good of the greatest number achieved as the result of the pursuit of enlightened self-interest by all, has become the unacknowledged principle behind modern democracy. But the development and survival of this principle has only been made possible by periodical interventions of the Puritan conscience whenever selfishness has predominated over enlightenment in the manifestations of enlightened self-interest. Benthamite principles were essentially the same as Leveller principles; the difference in the application of these principles as between Benthamites and Levellers is a reflection of the difference between the predominant material interests of the typical Benthamite on the one hand and the typical Leveller on the other. In the same way the similarity between the proposals in the Agreement of the People and the actual state of affairs in England to-day is indicative of the similarity between the material interests of the typical Leveller and those of the average voter in England to-day. In short, such different proposals and such different practices as arise out of a belief in the sovereignty of the people and in the existence of natural law and natural rights are due, not to differences in ideology, but to differences in the social status of those holding, and in a position to give practical effect to, these beliefs. Belief in the sovereignty of the people is in effect belief in the superior wisdom of people like oneself; such a belief only becomes democracy when the possibility of exercising effective power has, by means of civil disturbance or universal suffrage, penetrated sufficiently far down the social scale as to include in the expression 'people' a majority of the population.

Puritanism, so far from being imbued with any democratic or libertarian ideas, sought to impose an individual discipline based on revelation in place of the medieval collective discipline based on tradition. The Puritans inherited from the medieval Church the conviction of Original Sin, but they rejected the medieval remedy of compounding for Original Sin by collective obedience to the Church in favour of their own remedy (accessible only to the Elect) of individual Salvation.

Protestantism was not so much the channel through which the Renaissance flowed into Northern Europe as the dam which was erected in Northern Europe against the Renaissance. In Latin Europe the ideas of the Renaissance partly absorbed and partly were absorbed by the Church to form that compromise with paganism which is characteristic of modern Catholicism. In

Northern Europe the ideas of the Renaissance filtered through the dam of Protestantism and ultimately emerged in a variety of democratic and libertarian forms. In England Puritanism represented the left wing of Protestantism; the Levellers represented, not the left wing of Puritanism, but the advance guard—the premonitory trickle—of these rationalist and naturalist ideas which had been set in train by the Renaissance but dammed back by Protestantism.

Protestantism was at least as much a reaction against Renaissance paganism as it was against medieval Catholicism. The democratic and libertarian ideas which grew out of Protestantism were not nourished by Protestantism but rather developed in spite of Protestantism. They were coloured by Protestantism but represented an antithesis rather than a fulfilment of Protestantism.

Protestant Calvinism, as exemplified in English Puritanism, continued the medieval tradition of trying to mould human society in accordance with a preconceived idea of the Will of God, in opposition to the Renaissance concept of worshipping God seen as an idealization of man. Predestination, which was inherent but not predominant in medieval belief, was, as a result of the Calvinist rejection of the claim of the Church to interpret God's Will on earth, elevated into the principal instrument by which God's Will on earth was made manifest. The doctrine of Predestination was an insuperable barrier to the development of democratic and libertarian thought. It is only by regarding this doctrine as incidental to Puritanism that Puritanism can be regarded as a democratic or libertarian movement. If the doctrine of Predestination be regarded as of the essence of Puritanism, those ideas of liberty and democracy which appear at first sight as proceeding from Puritanism must be regarded as a protest against Puritan theology in the same way that Puritanism was a protest against medieval theology.

(Historically, Puritanism regarded itself as being a reversion to an older form and not as the development of a newer form of Christianity. The Puritans regarded themselves as reactionaries and not as progressives. It is a curious feature of nearly all English religious and secular movements of reform that their protagonists

93

have almost invariably based their case, not on the evolution of a new society, but on reversion to an old one. It was Thomas More, the Catholic, who thought in terms of Utopia. 'When Adam delved and Eve span, who was then the gentleman?' was an appeal, not to a future Utopia, but to a past age. Similarly the Levellers, in their arguments against the Independents, appealed, not to the future, but to the past.)

The Puritan was unable either to see nature in terms of God or God in terms of nature. He avoided the aberrations of paganism on the one hand and of atheism on the other at the cost of creating and perpetuating an antithesis between God and nature which both destroyed the authority of tradition and discredited the freedom born of that destruction. Hence Puritanism had no positive or direct influence either in rehabilitating old or in developing new lines of thought.

Although Puritanism was in origin an intellectual movement, its predominant influence was on action and not on thought. The doctrine of Predestination inhibited constructive thought but encouraged action. After the basic theological position of Puritan had become established, the function of Puritan thought was to act as an incentive to, and to justify the results of, Puritan action. (It is a mistake to suppose that the quality of action is conditioned by the purity of the stream of thought from which it proceeds. Generally speaking, original thought proceeds from men incapable of translating original thought into effective action; action proceeds from men incapable of using the results of thought except as a means of justifying action.)

The doctrine of Predestination was an intellectual dead-end; intellectual progress along the path taken by the Reformers was only possible after knocking down the barrier set up by Predestination. The doctrines of medieval Christianity could be regarded either as enrichments or as perversions of Christianity. Having taken the Puritan position of regarding them as perversions, it was inevitable that the doctrine of Predestination, which was not a Protestant invention but a selection from and an enlargement of medieval belief, should also come to be regarded as a perversion. Once Christianity is regarded as the religion of a

94

Book, as a static body of revelation which has periodically to be stripped of earthly accretions, it becomes difficult to make a universally acceptable distinction between the accretions and the revelation itself. Therefore Puritanism became regarded on the one hand as having destroyed a living growth and on the other hand as having called an arbitrary halt to a process of removing rubbish.

Nevertheless Puritanism retained, and retains, the empirical justification of providing a stimulus to virtue and a deterrent to vice. Puritanism can be viewed as an adaptation of the Ten Commandments to the requirements of English social life. And just as the Ten Commandments provided the Children of Israel with an ethical code which enabled them to fulfil the role of God's Chosen People, so the Puritan way of life provided the necessary stiffening and stimulus to the English people at the advent of an era of great economic opportunity.

The Puritan rejection of traditional disciplines and the barrier which Puritan beliefs (and particularly the Puritan belief in the literal inspiration of the Bible) placed in the way of the development of scientific thought, led inevitably to the evolution of a secular ethic based on conventions which were impervious both to the lessons of history and to the discoveries of science. Puritanism, which had started as a movement of extreme non-conformity, developed a tradition of almost exaggerated conformity to a set of conventions which Puritanism was able to impose on English middle-class life and which in sum came to comprise the middle-class ideal of respectability. The subtle difference between the French conception of 'comme il faut' and the English conception of 'respectable' illustrates both the deficiencies and the virtues of Puritanism. Respectability is an ideal inhibited by prudence; comme il faut is prudence elevated into an ideal. One can rise above respectability; one can only fall below comme il faut. Comme il faut suggests standards of taste; respectability imposes standards of behaviour. Comme il faut invites tolerance; respectability demands conformity. Comme il faut encourages thought but tends to inhibit action; respectability frowns on original thought but encourages action.

The Puritan wore his conventions with a difference. He wore them not as a shield but as a sword. He wore them not to make himself similar to other people but to make himself different from other people. They represented the ossification of his own beliefs, not the protective covering of other people's. So far from accepting them from society, he imposed them, to a large extent, on society. And with that imposition they became invested with a sort of sober flamboyance which found expression, amongst other things, in much of Victorian architecture.

The typical Puritan had tacitly abandoned the intellectual bases of his beliefs, and replaced them by conventions, long before these bases were eroded by the discoveries of science and by the onset of the Higher Criticism. The dominance of the Puritan ethic was destroyed, not by the erosion of its intellectual bases, but by the decay of the economic buttresses of its conventional façade. Towards the end of the eighteenth century the tide of Nonconformist Puritanism rose until it covered the upper middle class and lapped the feet of the aristocracy. A century later it began to fall back to its previous Nonconformist limits, leaving small, austere and salty pools behind it in the course of its ebbing.

The sharp distinction which is drawn in England between an intelligent man and an intellectual would seem to derive in part from the Puritan subjection of thought to serve the purposes of action. The intellectual concept of thought issuing in thought is, to the Puritan, a sterile concept. Faith is the only mental process which has any validity as a mental process. Thought, to become significant, must issue in action. This attitude of mind necessarily leads to a distrust of conclusions reached as a result of thought and a reliance on opinions held as a result of convention. It also necessarily means that opinions and habits are changed not as a result of thought but as a result of emotion.

Whereas the processes of reason are tested by scepticism, the processes of emotion can only be moderated by indifference. An emotion which is opposed to a convention is either defeated by or defeats a convention according to the extent to which that emotion is charged with indifference. A compromise is possible, but not a synthesis. The relegation of thought to the workshop and to the counting-house meant that private life became a matter of conventions and emotions. When the two were in alliance emotion sanctified convention; when the two were in opposition convention frustrated emotion.

This mental and emotional climate provided the incentive for material success and was only made tolerable by material success. Puritanism could only survive as the ethic of a materially successful class in which Puritanism provided the incentive for material success and material success the justification for Puritanism.

In the twentieth century Puritan respectability became not an offensive means of climbing to wealth and influence but a defensive means of trying to avoid falling into poverty and oblivion. 'Respectability' acquired a new connotation and came to imply the maintenance of respect for oneself rather than the extorting of respect from others. Puritanism was on the defensive and was concentrating not on the spreading of its influence upwards but on the avoidance of contamination from below.

If and when the tide turns again it will not turn as the result of an intellectual resurgence. Whether it turns as the result of a change of economic climate or as the result of a correlation between even more mysterious forces, the fact of the turn will generate its own intellectual justification and, in due time, its own conventional ethic.

CHAPTER VII

The Puritan Tradition and the Fine Arts

TWO basic Puritan beliefs conditioned the Puritan attitude towards the fine arts. First, the Puritan religious view of the relationship between spirit and nature prevented them from recognizing art as a bridge between spirit and nature and so denied to art any 'useful' function. Secondly, Puritan secular habit frowned on the idea of spending money and energies on pursuits which their religious beliefs taught them were superfluous.

To the Puritan, art was at best a decoration, an embellishment; he could not conceive it as part of the stuff of the good life. At worst it was a frivolous and meaningless dissipation of time, energy and money.

We are not concerned in this chapter with the effect on the Puritan character of this attitude to the fine arts; nor are we concerned with any effect on aesthetic theory of the Puritan attitude towards the fine arts, since aesthetic theory could hardly be affected by a philosophy which had no contact with aesthetics. All we are concerned with is the practical effect which Puritanism had on the development of the fine arts in England.

This practical effect can be considered under three main heads. First, the specific and disastrous effect which Puritanism has had on the development of the drama in England. Secondly, the effect which Puritanism has had on taste in the visual arts. Thirdly, the effect of Puritanism on the English attitude towards the fine arts in general.

The Puritan attitude to the drama was conditioned not only by those religious and secular beliefs which conditioned the Puritan attitude towards the arts in general. Puritans also had a number of specific objections to the drama based originally on the circumstances of the drama in Elizabethan times. First, there was the connection of the drama with the Miracle Plays, by means of which the beliefs of the medieval Church had been popularized and with the assistance of which the feasts of the medieval Church had been celebrated. Secondly, there was the Italianate habit of behaviour with which the Elizabethan drama was identified and which helped to account for the personal licentiousness of so many Elizabethan dramatists and patrons of the Elizabethan drama. Thirdly, there was the undoubted fact that in Elizabethan times dramatic performances were associated with immorality and rowdiness in much the same way as were Edwardian music halls.

The attitude of the Elizabethan Puritans succeeded in establishing the drama for the next 200 years as being in the same category as such sports as horse racing, cock fighting, and boxing—which were patronized by the aristocracy and the masses and frowned upon by the middle classes as being degrading both to the participants and to the onlookers.

As Puritan habits of life and thought penetrated both upwards and downwards during the first half of the seventeenth century, so both influential and popular support for the drama declined, with the natural result that the Puritan assessment of dramatists and actors and of the drama itself tended to approximate to the reality, in that the drama had to seek its support where it was most likely to find it. Under the Commonwealth, public dramatic performances were altogether forbidden. It is not surprising that the dramatic revival after the Restoration reflected both the repressions from which the drama had been suffering and the reputation with which the Puritans had endowed it.

One of the social effects of the Restoration was to segregate a large, able, and increasingly prosperous body of people, consisting of a fair proportion of the rising middle class, from any influence on or share in the main political and social activities of the time. This body consisted both of the Dissenters and of those who, while accepting the religious settlement for prudential reasons, disliked the cynicism and licence which were the inevitable results of that abandonment of both religious and political principle on which the Restoration was based. Thus it

was that English social, intellectual and religious life for the next
150 years proceeded along two parallel lines, until the wealth
and influence of the Dissenting and near- and ex-Dissenting
middle class enforced a coalescence with the descendants of the
beneficiaries of the Restoration. The politics, the art and the
social life of the eighteenth century must be viewed in the light
of this social, intellectual and religious divorce.

The result of this divorce, as far as the arts were concerned,
was to confine the patronage and appreciation of the arts to the
aristocracy and their hangers-on and to confirm in the rising
middle class a Puritan prejudice against the arts in general.
Consequently, the arts tended to be emasculated during the period
of the divorce and vulgarized afterwards. In particular—and this
applied especially to the drama—there grew up a conventional
antithesis between frivolity and good taste on the one hand, and
between seriousness and vulgarity on the other. The English
drama acquired the convention—which it has not wholly lost—
of confining itself to the depiction of contemporary upper-class
life. By the time middle-class influence had begun to reassert
itself in the arts, the tone and content of the English drama was
such as to confirm and to perpetuate Dissenting and Evangelical
prejudices.

With the rise of the Puritan tide in English life these prejudices
gained a considerable currency and had a variety of effects on
relations between the drama and the public. On the one hand the
drama adjusted itself to these prejudices by purging itself of
impropriety to such an extent that an uproar was caused less than
fifty years ago by the use of the word 'bloody' on the stage by a
character in one of Shaw's plays. (To-day the tide of propriety
has receded; the physical act of seduction can all but be shown
on the stage without adverse comment, and much current stage
dialogue is equally indecent with, although considerably less
witty than, the juiciest efforts of Farquahar or Wycherley.) On
the other hand theatregoing continued to be regarded as a dis-
reputable pursuit by many middle-class families until the last
years of the nineteenth century, when the influence of Queen
Victoria, who liked the theatre and was gracious to actors and

actresses, seems to have convinced all but the most austere that the 'legitimate' stage was in fact a legitimate source of respectable amusement. But, to the Puritan, it was, like other forms of art, only an amusement. It might be degrading, or it might, possibly, be elevating; but it could not, in any real sense of the word, be regarded as serious. The play of ideas which Bernard Shaw introduced into England did not appeal to Puritans, in spite of the title given by Shaw to one of his published series of plays. The essential Puritan attitude to the drama was not altered as a result of the drama conforming to the more obvious of the Puritan's moral prejudices. Essentially the Puritan regarded the drama in the same way as he regarded all the other arts—as an amusement, as a decoration, which might be incidentally elevating, but which was fundamentally insignificant.

The influence of Puritanism on taste in the visual arts was deeply affected by the cultural isolation, already referred to, which was imposed on Puritan sympathizers at the Restoration and which was not finally liquidated until the middle of the nineteenth century. The connection between Puritanism and philistinism probably derives as much from that isolation as it does from Puritan religious and secular beliefs. The pre-Restoration Puritan destroyed images in Churches because he objected to them theologically; the Victorian Puritan erected sham-Gothic monstrosities in Churches because he approved of them artistically. The seventeenth-century Puritan destroyed beautiful things because his outlook did not include an appreciation of sensual beauty; the nineteenth-century Puritan caused the creation of ugly things because his conventions had come to include a restrained respect for opulent ugliness. In his revolutionary days he was an iconoclast because his religion taught him to reject the symbolism of images; in his respectable days he preserved his rejection of symbolism by insisting on decoration which had no meaning whatever.

We have then to distinguish between the basic iconoclasm which dominated the Puritan attitude towards all visual art, and which resembled, for example, the attitude of the Wahhabi Moslem to-day, and the incidental philistinism which was the result of the super-imposition, first of cultural isolation, and then of opulence, on to the basic iconoclasm.

Art is only comprehensible as a serious reality if it is regarded as having, in intention, the sacramental quality of forming a bridge between the spirit and the sense. To a man who thinks in terms, not of connection between the spirit and the sense, but of subjugation of the one by the other, art can only avoid being blasphemous by being regarded as frivolous. When the Puritan took art seriously, he tried to destroy it; it was only by depriving it of meaning that he could be taught to tolerate it. This attitude obviously prevented him from regarding art as 'useful' within his conception of the meaning of the term. Art was at best the icing on the cake, the jam on the bread and butter.

This conception of art as being decorative, as being an optional extra, does not necessarily inhibit good taste in artistic matters. But sensitive appreciation of decorative art does demand a sympathy with the essential detachment and, to use the word in no pejorative sense, with the essential frivolity of such art. But the Puritan had no detachment and no frivolity. Art, even when regarded as an optional extra, must express something, and eighteenth-century visual art—the decorations of the brothers Adam and the paintings of Gainsborough, Reynolds and Constable for example—does express to perfection the agnostic detachment and ordered frivolity of eighteenth-century society. Puritanism had no part in this society. When Puritanism began, of its material superfluity, to indulge in optional extras, and when Puritans became artistic patrons, the art which they sponsored expressed solidity and earnestness as faithfully as the artistic productions of the eighteenth century expressed the very different qualities characteristic of their aristocratic patrons. Victorian taste was as unconscious of its social, economic and religious motivations as was eighteenth-century taste. The Victorian manufacturer, like the eighteenth-century aristocrat, knew what he liked and was prepared to pay for it. The Victorian merchant did not, any more than did the eighteenth-century aristocrat, put himself in the hands of a fashionable architect or interior decorator.

Visual art has a major and a minor function. Its major function

is, as has been said, to form a bridge between the spirit and the
sense. Its minor function is that of a period piece—to com-
municate to posterity something of the mind of the age in which
it was produced. Victorian visual art fulfils this minor function
in that it expresses the individual tastes of its sponsors. But in so
far as Victorian art fulfilled its minor function it failed to fulfil
its major function. In the context of Victorian taste, as dictated
by the Puritan middle class, the two functions were mutually
exclusive. For art to fulfil its major function it must be produced
by and for people who on the one hand can express and on the
other conceive the possibility of the interpenetration of the
senses by the spirit. The practice of the visual arts demands not
only artists but patrons. Literature and music cost nothing to
produce except the artist's time, and therefore can be produced,
if not sold, without the necessity for a patron. But buildings,
furniture, sculpture, jewellery, tapestries, and to some extent
paintings, involving the use of expensive materials, are not produced at all unless there are people prepared to commission them.
Consequently the visual arts, unlike literature and music, are
almost completely dependent on contemporary taste, and must
reflect the standards of contemporary taste. And contemporary
taste, in this connection, means the taste of those people with
sufficient money to purchase works of art for themselves, or with
sufficient influence to commission works of art for public bodies.

It is of course possible, and is to-day usual, for such people to
put themselves in the hands of professional advisers, like Parliament commissioning Mr. Graham Sutherland to paint the
portrait of Sir Winston Churchill. But the Victorian Puritan
would no more have taken his views on art from an artist than an
Elizabethan Puritan would have taken his views on religion from
a priest. The Puritan was essentially an individualist, even in
matters which he regarded as unimportant.

We now proceed to the third part of the enquiry undertaken
in this chapter, which is an examination of the effect of Puritanism
on the English attitude towards the fine arts in general.

The Puritan conception of art as an optional extra is a conception with which comparatively few Englishmen would be

inclined to quarrel, either in theory or in practice. In such matters of utility as town planning, house building and furniture designing there is a strong tendency to let the practical man do the essence of the thing and then, if at all, to get an artist to come along and add the frills. The proper domain of art, it is felt, is in the non-essential things, in the pleasant knick-knacks of life, in the poetry, in the jewellery, in the music, which a man can take or leave, which he does not have to live with, which are part of life's relaxations and not part of its serious business. In this domain the artist can do as he likes, just as the practical man can do as he likes in the serious matters. The artist is regarded partly as a public entertainer, like an actor or professional footballer, and partly as an ancillary professional man, like a chiropodist or a beauty specialist.

It is considered quite natural that artists among themselves should treat their work seriously, as do actors, professional footballers, chiropodists and beauty specialists; it is also considered quite natural that some people other than artists should take art seriously, in the same way as football fans take football seriously, and that most educated people should take an intelligent interest in art in the same way as they might take an intelligent interest in cricket. What is considered incomprehensible and unacceptable is any claim to regard the fine arts as part of the essential mechanism of life, like sex, or politics, or commerce, or religion. (For in England religion is still regarded as essential in theory, although in practice it has been relegated to the status of an optional extra.)

Is this attitude towards the fine arts an integral part of the English character, or is it an aspect of Puritanism which has been injected into the English character? It is suggested that this attitude is a residue—and an exceedingly persistent residue—of the Puritan cultural conquest of England during the nineteenth century.

One of the most remarkable things about this cultural conquest was the way in which it took possession of, moulded, and developed the Public School system, and thus impressed something of the Puritan morality on generations of ruling class males. The curious synthesis which was achieved, via the Public

School system, between classical studies, compulsory games and Puritan morality is a remarkable feature of English social life, and cannot possibly be neglected in any attempted assessment of the influence of Puritanism on English life as a whole. Some account of the influence of Puritanism on the Public School system has been reserved for this chapter since it is believed that a discussion of this subject in terms of the fine arts is peculiarly illustrative of the impact of Puritanism on the outlook of educated Englishmen in general.

It was only during the nineteenth century that the Public Schools became part of the system whereby the English ruling class was trained for the ever-increasing responsibilities which its members were being called upon to undertake. A number of ancient foundations had of course existed before the nineteenth century, but it was not until near the middle of the nineteenth century that a Public School education became regarded as an essential part of the upbringing of a ruling-class boy. By that time, and in order to meet the increasing demand, the handful of older Public Schools—Eton, Winchester, Westminster and so on—was being augmented both by the promotion of some of the older Grammar Schools and by the opening of new foundations.

As had happened with social customs in general, the rising manufacturing class both influenced and were influenced by the existing habits and customs which they adopted. Their vitality was such that they influenced these habits and customs more than they were influenced by them. But the effect of the Puritan impact was evolutionary rather than revolutionary; the process was one of infiltration rather than one of replacement.

In the eighteenth century the Dissenters had, through the medium of the Dissenting Academies, gone a long way towards developing their own autonomous system of education in England. In spite of their Utilitarian leanings, it had not occurred to them to confuse the process of education with the acquisition of useful knowledge, and the Dissenting Academies as a whole provided a classical education which compared favourably with that provided in Anglican establishments such as Eton and Winchester. When, with increasing success, influential Dissenters tended to revert to Anglicanism, they brought with them the educational ideas which had been nourished and developed in the Dissenting Academies. They realized, as the aristocracy and gentry did not realize, the necessity of training a ruling class for their duties by means of an organized system of education, and they grasped the fact that a classical education could be used as a discipline for training a man of affairs instead of being merely regarded as the equipment of a scholar or the ornament of a dilettante. It was this discovery which caused the Public School system to be rescued from the barbarity and squalor of people like Dr. Keate, and to be developed under the aegis of Headmasters like Dr. Arnold into a training-ground for those statesmen, legislators, leaders of commerce and industry, imperial administrators and so on, who were required in ever-increasing numbers, and of ever-increasing capacity, during the Victorian era.

The traditional system of the older Public Schools—monastic boarding establishments, classical education, and corporal punishment—was taken in hand and made into a conscious instrument for training the rulers of a mercantile and imperial people. The men who forged that instrument—of whom Dr. Arnold is the prototype—evolved a deliberate educational philosophy which was both adequate to the purposes which it was intended to serve and in sympathy with the views of those who sponsored the system. It was no accident that this philosophy was evolved principally by Evangelical clergymen whose social links with tradition and whose religious links with Puritanism rendered them ideal instruments for re-creating the Public School system for the performance of its new functions and for the service of its new patrons. The influence of the Evangelical Revival on the Public School system was among its most important and most permanent contributions to English life.

This Public School philosophy, evolved from these antecedents, has obviously exercised a dominating influence on English thought. This influence is now declining as a result both of a decline of the Public School monopoly as a training ground for responsibility and of the intrusion of other ideas into the Public Schools themselves.

The content of this philosophy was specifically Puritan. The culture of Athens was used to reinforce the ideals of Sparta; the language of Horace was used to inculcate the fear of Jehovah. Discipline was seen in terms not of sanctification but of repression. The rigours of the classroom and the vigours of the playing-field were dominated by a conviction of the menace of Original Sin. Everything that was not compulsory tended to be forbidden; everything that was spontaneous tended to be suspect. Scholarship in terms of the school curriculum, athletic prowess in terms of the school's compulsory games and personal piety in terms of Evangelical Christianity were the principal desiderata. Interests extraneous to these were discouraged.

What was being taught, and what was intended to be taught, was a view of the good life from which the fine arts were excluded. Beauty, as interpreted by Plato, Marcus Aurelius and St. Paul, was seen purely in terms of the soul. The Renaissance was viewed mainly in terms of the rediscovery of the Greek classics. The function of art as a means of interpreting nature in terms of spirit was outside the Public School philosophy, since this philosophy repudiated the relations between nature and spirit which this function implied. According to this philosophy, nature was almost a dirty word. Inevitably this philosophy led to interest in the fine arts being associated with effeminacy and in such interest being benevolently regarded only in so far as it was treated flippantly.

The Public School system did not, as has so often been charged, impose conformity. It inculcated a scale of values and encouraged a feeling of tolerant contempt for anything not comprised within it. This scale of values was rooted in the exaltation of the spirit over the flesh, in the exaltation of the will over the instinct, in the belief that action was the only respectable form of self-expression.

The encroachments of scientific discovery on the assumptions of Evangelical Christianity reinforced rather than weakened the Public School-Evangelical attitude towards the fine arts. For the scientists had no more use for the interpretative and reconciliatory functions of art than had the Puritans. But in a system committed as far as the Public School system was to Evangelical Anglicanism, it was inevitable that the Christian basis of belief should be more severely compromised than in the Anglican world at large, and the effect was to coarsen the Public School ethic into a Kipling-esque blend of sanctimoniousness and snobbery. The uncertainties of agnosticism replacing the serenity of Faith caused a different and less attractive attitude to be taken towards matters outside the average Public School man's comprehension; derision tended to replace tolerance and self-assertion to replace self-confidence.

(It is to be noted that the characteristic Puritan-Evangelical atmosphere of the Public Schools was not reproduced in the Universities, either in the two ancient foundations of Oxford and Cambridge, or in the newer 'provincial' Universities. Oxford and Cambridge had a traditional intellectual independence which prevented them from being used for the propagation of an essentially anti-intellectual philosophy; the newer Universities were intended to serve other purposes. The effect then of the Universities was to broaden and to liberalize, but not to eradicate, the outlook inculcated by the Public Schools.)

As with other aspects of the Puritan ethic, the Public School ethic was brought into being by the desire for material success, could only be justified by material success and was only either tolerable or tolerated in the light of material success. The 'old school tie' only became ridiculous, and the baser aspects of the Public School ethic only became conspicuous, when this ethic ceased to be the more or less exclusive passport to material success. The Public School system succeeded so well in producing the right kind of people who were needed to administer the responsibilities of nineteenth-century expansion, that the growth of the system continued without any relation to the needs of the demand to be supplied and without very much relation to the quality requirements of those needs. Thus a situation was created in which the Public School ethic degenerated into a conventional ideal of gentlemanliness quite unrelated to its original severely functional intention. This conventional ideal of gentlemanliness both minimized the qualities of will-power and application and exaggerated the defects of philistinism inherent in the Public School system. In short this convention magnified many of the vices and abandoned many of the virtues of the Puritanism from which it was derived. In so far as the fine arts were concerned, it perpetuated a specifically Puritan outlook which, mainly as a result of the Public School system, has been injected into English upper and middle-class life.

The attitude of a people towards the fine arts is best judged, not by the quality and quantity of the artistic productions of eminent practitioners, but by the extent to which artistic form is an integral and seemingly unconscious part of that people's utilitarian productions. Conscious preoccupation with such matters as industrial design and town-planning is a sure indication that artistic form is an afterthought rather than an intrinsic part both of industrial design and of town-planning. Do such things really matter except in so far as deficiencies in industrial design may affect our export trade to countries more sensitive about these things? Is the lack of feeling for artistic form any more than the incidental lack of a comparatively unimportant quality (after all one can't have everything), or is it a symptom of a deeply rooted malaise which has much wider consequences than the building of ugly suburbs and the production of hideous furniture? These are questions to which there is no definitive answer. They are put here in order to suggest the possible scope both of the deficiencies and of the qualities of the Puritan contribution to English life. On the one hand the Puritan tradition has endowed the English people with strength of will, application of mind, energy of body and a deep sense of responsibility. On the other hand, it is suggested, the Puritan tradition has resulted in a widespread and deep-rooted indifference to and even contempt for the element of beauty in the world of man and, it may be added, in the human relations between man and man. The fact that Puritanism is only an element and, possibly, a minor element, both in the English tradition and in the make-up of the average educated English individual makes the Englishman both uncertain about the qualities and uneasy about the defects. The only practical purpose in trying to analyse the Puritan tradition is to attempt to isolate both the qualities and the defects with a view to pointing out the desirability of encouraging the one and of discouraging the other. For the Puritan *per se* there is no choice. The defects go with the qualities, just as a Jersey cow produces good milk and poor meat. But a farmer breeding from a variety of stocks can exercise a choice and can, if he breeds wisely, get the balance of qualities that he requires. Always of course supposing that balance is a desirable characteristic. For human happiness it is almost certainly desirable. For human achievement a certain element of unbalance to serve as a spur to action would seem to be indispensable. Happy men are apt to produce nothing except their own kind. For a man to leave nothing to clear up after him presupposes an existence of remarkable inactivity. Let it not be forgotten that the practice of the fine arts is only made possible by the activity of those whose activity often precludes them from sharing or even from understanding the benefits conferred by the fine arts which the fruits of their activity have made possible.

CHAPTER VIII

The Flower of the Puritan Tradition;
Gladstone and Gordon

THE view has been expressed in these pages that Puritanism in England, nipped in the bud by the failure of the Puritan Revolution in the seventeenth century, came to a second flowering in the nineteenth century, when the middle-class manufacturers and business men, many of them Dissenters and ex-Dissenters who had been reared in the Puritan tradition, rose to power and influence. The qualities and defects, the certainties and doubts of nineteenth-century Puritanism are exhibited *in excelsis* in the lives of two of the greatest of Victorian figures—William Ewart Gladstone and Charles George Gordon.

Both exhibited to a superabundant degree the characteristic Puritan qualities of piety and energy. Both were convinced that their actions were in accordance with the Will of God, and both constantly sought Divine guidance in prayer. Both combined external self-righteousness with internal self-questioning. Both were tortured throughout their lives by the Puritan conception of the antithesis between spiritual and material things. In both of them intense desire for, struggled with no less self-contempt for desiring, the world's approbation and the world's rewards.

Both were born into sufficiently easy circumstances as to be untroubled with the need for making money. Neither appears to have been seriously troubled by the spectacle of social and economic inequality. Both gave a large part of what they had to charity, and in both personal charity took unconventional forms which were probably manifestations of their inner conflicts. Gordon's habit of dispensing charity to small boys was as liable to misconstruction as was Gladstone's lifelong practice of per-sonally endeavouring to reclaim prostitutes. While there is no suggestion whatever of impropriety, there is little doubt that these activities, perhaps unconsciously, provided each of them with some emotional compensation for the emotional strains and stresses to which each of them subjected himself.

Gladstone was a type of nineteenth-century conformist and Gordon of nineteenth-century nonconformist Puritanism. This conformity and this nonconformity were, according to the nineteenth-century Puritan pattern, exhibited not so much in their religious beliefs as in their secular achievements. Gladstone attained the apogee of conventional achievement, Gordon the apogee of unconventional fame.

William Ewart Gladstone was born in 1809 in Liverpool. His father, John Gladstone, was a prominent merchant of that city. He was of Scottish descent and had come to England from Edinburgh in early manhood. Born a Presbyterian and a Whig, he graduated with success to becoming an Anglican and a Tory, like so many of the rising middle-class magnates of that time. The Gladstone home was strongly Christian and strictly Evangelical.

Charles George Gordon was born in 1833 into not dissimilar surroundings. On his father's side he came of a military family of Scottish descent; on his mother's side he came of a family of wealthy English shipowners. Gordon's home, like Gladstone's, was strongly Christian and strictly Evangelical.

In his religious observance Gordon remained all his life within the Evangelical tradition although, towards the end of his life, he began, when the means were available, to take the Sacrament more often than was usual for an Evangelical, and he is recorded as having written that the High Church party was 'more in the right direction than the Low'. Gladstone became a High Churchman, but he wore his High Churchmanship, like he wore everything else, with a difference, and he was certainly much nearer in temperament to the Evangelicals than he ever was to the Puseyites.

Gladstone was temperamentally a scholar who was driven to a life of action both by an ambition which was all the more devouring as the result of his refusal to acknowledge it, and by that Puritanical compulsion which insisted on action as the only legitimate fruit of thought. Gordon was temperamentally a man of action who was driven to theological and metaphysical speculation as the result of his anguished awareness of what, in terms of his religious beliefs, he could only regard as the barren fruits of his actions.

The two men never, so far as is known, met. One feels that Gladstone would have been interested in the Palestine researches undertaken by Gordon just before his last expedition to Khartoum, although he would almost certainly have quarrelled violently with Gordon's conclusions. It seems improbable that Gordon, who was not a classical scholar, would have displayed very much interest in Gladstone's Homeric studies. But the scholastic approach of the two men was similar in spite of the great difference in intellect between them. Gladstone approached Homer, as Gordon approached the Holy Land, with the determination to find something which he had already decided was there.

Gladstone's mental equipment enabled him, by refinements and subtleties of casuistry which have baffled historians and biographers, in some sort to solve the inner conflicts inherent in his nature and to a large extent to harness his religious beliefs to the necessities of a political career. Gordon had no such intellectual resources and in consequence his frustrated external life was the mirror of his unresolved internal conflicts.

This difference in intellectual power explains Gladstone's success and Gordon's failure in equating the impulses of their own strong wills with their conception of the Divine Will. To an ever-increasing extent during the course of his long life, Gladstone avoided on the one hand what he would have regarded as the frustration of submitting his will to that of God, and on the other hand what he would have regarded as the impiety of consciously neglecting the Will of God, by persuading himself of an identity between his own and the Divine Will. Gordon, like Gladstone, regarded submission as frustration and neglect as impiety, but, unlike Gladstone, was always acutely conscious of opposition between his own and the Divine Will. Each had too much pride to submit to God without a sense of frustration and too much conscience to neglect God without a sense of sin. Gladstone found a way out; Gordon did not. Gladstone's success has caused him, not without some justice, to be branded as a humbug; Gordon's failure has caused him, not without some reason, to be lauded as a saint. But in truth Gladstone stopped short of being a humbug by about the same measure as Gordon stopped short of being a saint. Gladstone never consciously abandoned his principles; Gordon never wholly abandoned his pride. Both were too much in the Puritan tradition to attain sufficient humility or sufficient cynicism as to make such abandonment possible.

There was a volcanic unpredictability about both men which was more characteristic of seventeenth-century than of nineteenth-century Puritanism. It was at all events sufficiently strong and sufficiently near the surface as to make many sober people wonder at times whether either Gordon or Gladstone was entirely sane. But there were many more equally sober people, to whom the extravagances of Puritanism were more familiar and more sympathetic than is generally the case to-day, who almost literally worshipped Gladstone while he was alive and Gordon after he was dead. For beneath the respectable and (to use a phrase of Lord Northcliffe's) 'money-logged' exterior of nineteenth-century Puritanism there still existed that elemental 'fire in the belly' which is at once the saving grace and the practical nuisance of the Puritan faith. Posterity appreciates the saving grace in its estimate both of Gladstone and of Gordon. Contemporaries recognized both the saving grace and the practical nuisance.

The closing epic of Gordon's life which, by its ending, blasted Gladstone's political reputation, shows Gladstone at Hawarden and Gordon at Khartoum, each in a passion of rage with the other, each trying to force contradictory policies on the other, and each convinced that he was the chosen instrument of God for the fulfilment of His Purposes on earth. This struggle of will between two obstinate and tortured men, each communing with God in prayer and each making copious daily entries in his private journal, the one unconsciously encompassing the death, and the other, perhaps less unconsciously, encompassing the disgrace, of the other, marks the approximate chronological end of the Puritan middle-class domination of Victorian England. The somewhat similar disagreements which festered between Lloyd George and Haig a generation later were conducted in a very different idiom.

A man who sincerely regards his actions as directly guided by God is almost certain to attribute diabolic motives to his opponents, to see disagreements in terms of a battle between good and evil. When one is at war with an enemy this attitude is perhaps not a bad thing. When one is merely at variance with a colleague its advantages are less apparent. In the tragedy of Khartoum each of the principal protagonists was inclined to attribute diabolic motives to the other. (It is fascinating to consider the impassive Baring, who had in him more of the intellectual clarity of the eighteenth century than the moral fervour of the nineteenth, trying to evolve a coherent policy out of the serpentine evasions of Mr. Gladstone on the one hand and the impetuous contradictions of General Gordon on the other.) This attribution both motivated and provided self-justification for the deceptions practised by the one and the delays imposed by the other. It is almost certainly correct to say that each viewed the Mahdi with more respect and with more sympathy than he regarded his domestic opponent.

Cast together as principals in the tragedy of Khartoum they were both at their worst, because they were acting in roles in which neither of them really believed. Gladstone regarded the whole Egyptian question as a tiresome problem bequeathed to him by the previous Government; Gordon had no illusions about the quality of the Egyptian rule he was trying to preserve in the Sudan. They were each faced with the uncongenial necessity of having to make the best of a choice between two evils. On Gordon's side there was no opportunity for offensive action; on Gladstone's side there was no great moral principle to be implemented. Gordon was in the centre of the stage with no opportunity for action; Gladstone was in a subordinate role with no opportunity either for administration or for oratory. But the mere fact of opposition gave a moral content to expediency. When one considers the well-known story of Gladstone's anger as he read a sensational newspaper report (inspired by Gordon) about some of Gordon's despatches from Khartoum, one is irresistibly reminded of Wilde's epigram about the rage of Caliban at seeing his own face in the glass. For Gordon's method of using moral reprobation as a means of whipping up popular indignation was not dissimilar from Gladstone's own. Gordon from Khartoum was using against Gladstone the same methods as Gladstone himself had used in Midlothian against Disraeli. Gordon, with his apparently guileless simplicity, had manœuvred himself into a position in which he was bound to win. He either gained a martyr's crown or converted the British Government to his own policy in the Sudan. Gladstone, with his subtle refinements, had been manœuvred into a position in which he was bound to lose. He would be forced either to adopt Gordon's policy in the Sudan or go down to posterity as having abandoned Gordon. In his efforts to avoid this tiresome choice he found himself both committed to the one and doomed to the other.

The opinion has been indicated in these pages that the basic defect of Puritanism was its inability to provide a bridge between spirit and nature and so bring harmony to the individual soul. The strength of Puritanism undoubtedly lay in the applicability of the Puritan ethic to business and public life, and in the force and fire which the Puritan ethic bestowed on those who did apply it to business and public life. The self-questionings of Puritanism tortured men in contemplation, but its certainties fortified them in action. The austerities of Puritanism set up hideous tensions in times of leisure, but trained men for endurance in times of peril. The individualism which was inculcated by Puritanism made men unsympathetic as colleagues but self-reliant as leaders. The sense of responsibility which was characteristic of Puritanism made men self-righteous in counsel but meticulous in performance. The strength of will which was the essence of Puritanism sometimes made men stubborn in the face of reason but always made them inflexible in the face of adversity.

In both Gladstone and Gordon the Puritan ethic applied to their particular metiers—Gladstone's finance and Gordon's soldiering—provided the elements of conviction, daring and

force which made the difference between talent and genius, the
difference between contemporary respect and immortal fame.
When Gladstone was preparing and delivering his Budgets, or
when Gordon was waging his campaigns in the valley of the
Yang-tse, the volcanic passions which at other times threatened
to erupt as public and private nuisances, were harnessed and
canalized to provide an irresistible flow of reasoning power,
resolution and resource. When they were not the servants of
these particular metiers, these volcanic passions were apt to
assume the mastery and to envelop their subjects in clouds of
caprice, self-deception, righteous indignation, mock humility
and a quite remarkable insensitiveness to the feelings and prejudices of others.

CHAPTER IX

The Decline of the Puritan Tradition

IT is possible to regard Puritanism, in its various stages of religious protest, political revolt and social success, as a phenomenon peculiar to those 350 years of English history which divide the collectivism of the medieval from the collectivism of the modern State. It can be regarded as an integral part of that process of religious, political and social evolution which began with the Wars of the Roses and ended with the First World War (in so far as such a process can be said to have a definite beginning and a definite end).

The religious, intellectual, economic and social climate of the nineteenth century in England, which had originally been imposed by, and subsequently both sustained and was sustained by the Puritan middle class, was based on religious fundamentalism, intellectual certainty, economic individualism and social austerity. During the last years of the nineteenth century this climate showed many indubitable signs of change. This change was not due merely to a slackening of the various high tensions which are inherent in the Puritan way of life, which had been screwed to their highest pitch during the previous half century and which could not in any case have been indefinitely maintained. It was also due to the emergence of other, positive modes of thought brought into being by changing economic circumstances, new intellectual fashions and new scientific discoveries.

The successful assaults made both by scientific discovery and by 'Higher Criticism' of the Bible had begun gravely to compromise the Puritan religious position in the sixties and seventies of the nineteenth century. The Puritan belief in the literal inspiration of the Bible derived naturally from the Puritan denial of any authority inhering in the Church or in the priesthood. In practice, individual judgment required the sanction of some external and infallible authority, and the Bible became regarded to an increasing extent as such an authority. (General Gordon probably referred to the Bible more frequently than Oliver Cromwell for guidance in the practical affairs of life.) The assaults made on this belief struck at the very heart of the Puritan religion, since it was more difficult for the Puritan than for the Catholic to accept anything in the nature of an allegorical explanation of parts of the Bible.

The effect of this successful attack on fundamentalism was to increase Catholic as opposed to Evangelical influence in Anglican circles and to shift the attention of Nonconformists away from theological and towards social questions by a process analogous to that which had accompanied the decline of Calvinist beliefs in Nonconformist circles during the eighteenth century. The result was a retreat from individualism in both cases; in Anglican circles this retreat took the form of a return towards traditionalism, in Nonconformist circles an advance towards collectivism.

Less obviously, and more insidiously, damaging to Puritanism than the attack on Puritan fundamentalist religion was the tendency towards pragmatism which was becoming apparent in English secular thought. The old conception of absolute Truth determined either by revelation or by reason was giving way to a relative conception of truth as a series of individual hypotheses which provided a coherent and constant relation between observed phenomena. The old certainties were dissolving. From regarding truth as a question of hypothesis it was but a short step to regarding conduct as a matter of expediency. From a climate in which economic theories and social customs were regarded as eternal verities English society was entering a climate in which the eternal verities were being degraded to the status of theories and customs to be tested in the light of experiment and of expediency.

The essential Puritan position was based on the assertion of individualism *vis-à-vis* collectivism in both religious and secular affairs. The doctrine of *laissez faire* was a secular statement of this essential position. Such inroads as had been made into this doctrine, chiefly in the form of State regulation of conditions of employment and State provision of certain social services, had been counterbalanced by the almost mystical importance which came to be attached to Free Trade, and had not affected what appeared to be its essential impregnability.

It is difficult to discern the exact date at which the practical desirability of regulating certain aspects of *laissez faire* began to be accompanied by a positive belief in the virtue of State-control as such. The process of conversion was accelerated by numerous factors, some purely domestic, some global. Among the domestic factors was the progressive enfranchisement of the workers, whose method of social and economic advancement by means of social legislation and by bargaining through their Trade Unions was seen in terms not of individualism but of collectivism. Among the global factors the effect on manufacturers both of increasing foreign competition and of the increasing power of the Trade Unions caused them to abandon both their traditional Free Trade principles in favour of some form of Protection and their traditional individualism in favour of Federations for offering resistance to the Unions and for applying pressure to the Government.

(The move towards collectivism was masked by the continued, although qualified, adherence of the Liberal Party, in spite of its reliance on the votes of the newly-enfranchised workers, to the Gladstonian and Puritan principles of Free Trade, free enterprise and public economy. *Laissez faire* as an element in public policy died with the effective demise of the Liberal Party; by the third decade of the twentieth century both the Conservative and the Labour Parties saw the State primarily as an agency for the prosecution of the economic interests of the supporters of the Party in power.)

At the beginning of the twentieth century the principal pillars of *laissez faire*—Free Trade and low taxation—were being eroded by the demands of manufacturers, sponsored by the Conservative Party, for some form of fiscal protection, and by the demands of the workers, sponsored by the Liberal and later by the Labour Party, for increased social services provided out of taxation.

But this slow process of erosion was a much less important

factor in changing the prevailing economic climate of *laissez faire* than the economic imperialism and the heavy armaments expenditure which resulted from the growing economic rivalry between the established British industrial empire and the growing industrial empires of the United States and Germany. These growing industrial empires were—as a result of Great Britain's previous virtual monopoly of overseas markets for manufactured goods—in direct competition with, and in a greater or lesser degree hostile to, Great Britain. The British reaction to this competition and to this hostility was to start thinking in terms of regarding the British Empire as a single economic unit whose united resources and united potentialities would offset the effect of this competition and of this hostility. This reaction led to an enlargement of the strategic conceptions both of Great Britain and of her rivals, and to a policy of aggression and of counter-aggression in the 'colonial' areas of Africa, China and Australasia. The result was increased expenditure on armaments, and particularly on naval armaments, by all concerned (a development which was by no means unwelcome to the big iron and steel interests in all the competing empires), increased taxation and an increased sense of community between the activity of industry and the policy of the State. In England this development had a great effect in hastening the revision of that relationship between the individual and the State, based on the doctrine of *laissez faire*, which had been the basis of Victorian prosperity. But in Germany this development resulted in a logical extension of the principles on which the Prussian State had already established its domination over Central Europe.

The Prussianized German Empire owed its intellectual and industrial dominance to qualities which were the antithesis of those qualities of individualism and contempt for authority which had contributed so powerfully to the dominance of nineteenth-century England. The Prussian ideal was one of the conscious subordination of the individual to the State; its mode of operation was one which, to the nineteenth-century Englishman, would have seemed a contradiction in terms—a democratically elected and despotic Government.

Prussian efficiency and the congruence of Prussian intellectual theories with the organization of the German State and with the realities of German policy exercised a considerable attraction on English minds during the closing years of the nineteenth century, before German competition had graduated from the status of a problem to that of a menace, and contributed powerfully towards the dissolution of that individualist Victorian climate which was the apotheosis of English Puritanism.

Simultaneously with, and perhaps conditioned by, these changes in religious, philosophical and economic climate, a considerable change was becoming apparent in the social life and social outlook of the English middle class. This change is seen at its most characteristic in the changing habit of the middle class in the matter of recreation. Typical Puritan recreations, in so far as they were taken at all, partook of the same seriousness and strenuousness which characterized the Puritan approach to work and to religion. The Puritan tradition had always frowned on games and sports, mainly because they were associated in the Puritan mind either with Sabbath-breaking or with unseemly levity between the sexes. When increasing prosperity brought the opportunities and temptations of leisure, Puritan austerity developed suitably sober means of occupying leisure and finding a vent for overflowing energy in such pursuits as walking, mountain-climbing, nature-study, sketching, amateur carpentry and so on. Most of these pursuits became invested in the Puritan mind with either a practical or a moral purpose. The whole idea of amusement or recreation as a relaxation, as a 'change', as a means of 'killing time', was abhorrent to the Puritan mind. 'If I but seek oblivion of a day, so shorten I the stature of my soul.' This attitude dictated the attitude of the Puritan to his recreations (which he would not have demeaned by considering or by referring to as 'amusements'). The word 'amusing', regarded as an adjective of approbation, would have been particularly distasteful to the typical Puritan. The moral aura with which cricket and football became surrounded in the Public Schools was a characteristic Puritan development and arose as a result of the Evangelical tone cultivated by the Public Schools during the nineteenth century. Anything less frivolous than the system of compulsory games at a Public School is difficult to imagine.

The development of amusements as an integral and ever-increasing part of English middle-class life dates from the seventies. Games such as croquet, lawn tennis, bowls and, later, golf started to become part of the normal routine of middle-class life. The old middle-class prejudice against the theatre began to die out, and attendance at horse races began to become almost respectable. Visits to seaside watering-places, which had been previously considered slightly raffish, began to become established as a conventional form of middle-class holiday. Amusing relaxations were taking the place of purposeful recreations. Most of these relaxations involved an increased freedom of intercourse between the sexes, whereas the old middle-class recreations had been almost exclusively male. The avowed aim of these relaxations was amusement; it was no longer considered necessary to invent a moral purpose for them.

All these developments, religious, philosophical, economic and social, partly destructive of old, and partly constructive of new, ways of thought and methods of action combined together during the last decade of the nineteenth and the first decade of the twentieth century to change that characteristic climate which is known as Victorianism and which, according to the argument of this book, represented the high-water-mark of Puritan influence on English life. The 1914-18 war can conveniently be regarded as the crucible both in which the Puritan way of life was dissolved and in which the dominant economic individualism of the middle class was finally destroyed. It can also be conveniently regarded as marking the approximate end of a process of religious, philosophical, economic and social development which started with the Reformation and which was based on the validity of individual judgment, on the inevitability of material progress and on the certainty of Divine Retribution. These three certainties invested Puritanism with its characteristic qualities of will, of confidence and of conscience. The energies of Puritanism can be seen in terms of the unison of these three certainties; the tensions of

Puritanism can be seen in terms of the inevitable oppositions between them.

The certainties which nourished Puritanism have all but dissolved into thin air; the fears which tormented Puritans have become meaningless to the vast majority of people. The virtues of Puritanism are no longer believed to ensure either prosperity in this world or Salvation in the next. Theologically and economically Puritanism has become discredited.

Puritanism was not wholly or even mainly the product of a certain theological and economic climate; but that theological and economic climate was necessary for its development. Puritanism was a conscious and onerous discipline which depended for its continued observance, and still more for its authority, upon the effective existence of certain material incentives and of certain spiritual beliefs. But a discipline, long persisted in, creates certain ineradicable habits and quasi-beliefs which continue after the discipline has been consciously abandoned. Puritanism can be distinguished to-day in the residual habits and quasi-beliefs with which it has marked the life of the English people and particularly the life of the English middle class.

Puritanism was always peculiarly a middle-class way of life, bound up with the emergence, struggles and, finally, with the dominance of the middle class. It was under the stimulus of Puritanism as a religion, as an ethic, and as a social habit that the middle class activated and controlled first the commercial, then the industrial, and finally the political, professional and social life of England. Simultaneously with the disappearance of Puritanism as a dominant force, there disappeared as a distinctive entity that class which had become identified with Puritanism. To-day the term 'middle class', in so far as it means anything, is only a statistical expression. There is no distinctive, homogeneous middle class. The broad division in England to-day is between those who are nett contributors to, and those who are nett beneficiaries of, direct taxation. In so far as the Puritan tradition continues to exist at all, it exists only in the former group, among which is included the descendants of the Victorian middle class, inextricably mixed with *déraciné* aristocracy and gentry on the one hand and with the more successful descendants of the Victorian working class on the other. The only thing held in common by this heterogeneous group is a common support for the Conservative Party, which reflects this heterogeneousness in its lack of any coherent principle beyond a general desire to limit the incidence of direct taxation so far as is compatible with the political necessity of obtaining the votes of a sufficient number of the other—and numerically much larger—group. Within this group Puritanism survives—in so far as it survives at all—both as vestiges of beliefs and as vestiges of habits.

In this connection it is necessary to consider the social phenomenon known as the Nonconformist conscience, which in some sort can be considered as a residual survival of Puritanism and which, even to-day, still exerts some influence.

It has already been noted that one result of the Evangelical Revival in the Church of England, and of the influence of Methodism on Dissent, had been to bring the Church of England and Dissent nearer together in a common enthusiasm for Evangelical Christianity. This on the one hand facilitated the passage of many Dissenters back into the Church of England, and on the other hand helped to create that common social outlook between middle-class Anglicans and middle-class Dissenters which was a characteristic feature of the Victorian era.

The factors which we have discussed and which led to the gradual dissolution of Puritanism towards the end of the century operated particularly powerfully on the upper, that is to say the Anglican, levels of the Victorian middle class, who were more exposed than the general run of Dissenters to the distractions of wealth, to the speculations of science and philosophy, to the economics of international trade, and to the seduction of aristocratic and continental fashions. Thus it came about that Puritanism tended to ebb from Anglicanism, just as it had risen into Anglicanism, as a result of a change in economic circumstances and social and intellectual attitudes, and returned to its previous status as the distinguishing mark of Dissent. But it was Puritanism with a difference. It had shed its distinctive Calvinism. Economically and politically it was on the defensive against collectivism—the collectivism of Big Business as well as the collectivism of the Trades Unions—instead of being on a victorious offensive against oligarchy. Religiously and socially it was on the defensive against scientific humanism and against agnostic hedonism instead of being on the victorious offensive against apathy and corruption. It had lost both its religious certainties and its economic justifications. Its essential bases were compromised by the increasing materialism of Nonconformist religion and by the increasing collectivism of Nonconformist politics, which were inextricably wedded with the social gospel of radical Liberalism. The history of eighteenth-century Nonconformity was repeating itself. Nevertheless, as in the eighteenth century, Puritan habits of behaviour persisted in Nonconformity, and at one time it seemed possible that these habits would influence the rising political forces of the twentieth century as powerfully as they had influenced the rising political forces at the beginning of the nineteenth century. But the social and intellectual climate was not propitious and the rising Labour movement moved steadily away from its early Nonconformist and Puritan associations. Belief in Original Sin, however attenuated, and resistance to the authority of the State, however modified by advocacy of State social services, did not sort well with a movement grounded in the belief that vice was the result of bad social conditions and based on the advocacy of State control of the principal means of production. Thus the last stronghold of Puritanism came to be associated with that largely Nonconformist section of the lower-middle-class which was being ground economically between the upper mill-stone of Big Business 'rationalization' and the nether mill-stone of working-class collectivism. Politically, this class was associated with the Liberal Party, whose eventual virtual extinction was basically due to its failure to obtain mass support for the combination of economic individualism, social service and personal austerity which was exhibited by the Nonconformist conscience.

To this extent the decline of the Puritan tradition can be associated with the decline of the Liberal Party. Towards the end of the nineteenth century Puritanism became reassociated with

Nonconformity in the way we have described; at the same time Liberalism became associated with Nonconformity as a result of the enfranchisement of the lower-middle-class and the defection of the aristocracy and upper-middle-class from Liberalism. Thus Puritanism and Liberalism came together in an accidental alliance which was cemented by the bitter disputes between Conservatives and Liberals and between Church and Dissent over the 1902 Education Act. But this very dispute, in which the Nonconformists advocated State-controlled and State-financed secular education, was indicative of the extent to which Nonconformity had departed from Puritan principles. It was also indicative of the extent to which the old Puritan principles of self-help and individualism were becoming submerged in what was to become the basic question in twentieth-century domestic politics—a competition to obtain the maximum possible share of the benefits of State assistance, while making the minimum possible contribution towards these benefits.

In the atmosphere of this enervating competition, Nonconformist Puritanism degenerated into a series of rearguard actions against the encroachments of the 'Continental Sunday' and a series of sporadic campaigns in favour of the extension of existing licensing and anti-gambling laws. Militant Puritanism had become identified with the resentful protests of a section of the lower-middle-class which had lost both the religious faith and the individual self-reliance which would have given a certain immediate dignity and a probable ultimate success to their protests.

Effective protests against the abuses of authority must be motivated by coherent and communicable principles and sustained by a conscious and infectious integrity. Effective exercise of authority must be motivated by the same principles and sustained by the same integrity. We have seen Puritanism in protest and Puritanism in authority. We have seen how the effectiveness of Puritanism both in protest and in power has been dependent on the maintenance of these principles and of this integrity. We have seen how a departure from these principles and from this integrity has led to ineffectiveness both in protest and in power. Is the current neglect of Puritan principles and the current departure from Puritan integrity due to a decline in Puritan virtues or is it due to the fact that these principles and this integrity no longer have any validity in the light of modern knowledge and of modern circumstances? There is no certain answer to these questions.

Looking back, Puritanism may be likened to a vein of hard rock running through the soil of our national history, sometimes at varying depths below the surface, sometimes outcropping. Where it outcrops, the countryside is harsh and austere; no soft and shady places for relaxation or dalliance; no verdure to rest, nor bright colours to delight, the eye; but a countryside rich in durable building materials, a countryside where the ring of the hammer is more familiar than the sound of laughter, where the houses have the air of fortresses, and where the keen air braces and sustains men for the work which they have set themselves to do.

CHAPTER X

The Anatomy of Puritanism

'Whereas the Catholics and the Anglicans had accepted the whole man, his primitive instincts, his inevitable response to sensuous beauty, his imagination, his playfulness, his laughter, the Calvinists attempted to reduce man to a reasoning machine, rational both in response and in expression. But under the long faces, the black hats, the sober clothes, in the midst of pious expressions of Calvinist dogma, still beat the forces of passion, the yearning for beauty, and a whole psychology of forces too powerful for Calvinism to resist or wholly degrade. Hence the long gap between Sabbath preachments and nightly yearnings, the hypocrisies, the repressions, the burning hatreds, the almost savage insistence on the letter of dogma. In their souls raged a perpetual conflict between the world of the senses and the stern discipline of the Old Testament creed, futilely diluted with the tolerant charity of the Gospels. Neither the deepest recesses of the Puritan soul nor its brightest will ever be probed; the complexities are too many, the variations too diverse.'

Extract from *Milton in the Puritan Revolution*, by Don M. Wolfe.

SHAKESPEARE had reason to know and to dislike the Puritans of his time; they did their best to prevent him from earning a living. He paints the darker side of Puritanism in his character of Angelo in *Measure for Measure*; he paints the ridiculous side in his character of Malvolio in *Twelfth Night*.

Taken by themselves, there was nothing particularly reprehensible in Angelo's lust for Isabella, nor ridiculous in Malvolio's amorous pretensions to Olivia. Taken by themselves, there was nothing reprehensible in Angelo's persecuting zeal, nor ridiculous in Malvolio's sombre dignity. It was the combination of lust and persecution that was reprehensible in Angelo, and of amorous pretensions and sombre dignity that was ridiculous in Malvolio. Both the persecuting zeal and the sombre dignity were reactions from the natural lusts of the one and from the natural vanity of the other, adopted in obedience to a belief which, instead of trying to civilize the natural passions of lust and vanity, tried to overcome them with an effort of the will. One suspects that Angelo could only have overcome his lust for Isabella by being even more tyrannical towards the frailties of other people, and that Malvolio could only have overcome his love for Olivia by imposing an even more straitlaced régime on Olivia's household.

The medieval mind was at least as much obsessed with sin and its consequences as was the Puritan mind. The fear of hellfire was just as much of an insistent reality in the medieval as it was in the Puritan soul. But the medieval man, being, like the modern man, a collectivist, dealt with the problem of sin in much the same way as the modern man deals with the problem of material misfortune. He insured against the worst consequences of sin as the modern man insures against the worst consequences of material misfortune. The modern man arranged this insurance through the State; the medieval man arranged his insurance through the Church. The medieval Church, in one of its many aspects, represented an elaborate system of universal insurance against the punishments—in this world and the next—imposed by medieval theology on the results of human frailty.

Puritanism abandoned the medieval system of insurance, but retained the medieval theology. This combination of medieval theology with individual liability goes far to explain both the heroisms and the hypocrisies, the austerities and the yearnings, the conscious solemnities and the unconscious fooleries, the repressions and the rancours, the ecstasies and the aridities, which characterize Puritanism.

It can be argued that the practices of the medieval Church grew up as a defence mechanism against the assumptions of medieval theology; alternatively it can be argued that medieval theology was built up in order to create a need for the spiritual facilities provided by the medieval Church. In either case it is clear that the practices of the medieval Church, and the relation in which medieval man stood to the medieval Church, are only explicable in the light of medieval theology.

The Church dispensed Absolution in return for faith and obedience because, in the light of the fears which dominated medieval religious belief, the assurance of Absolution was, for most men, a condition of any bearable earthly existence. Faith and obedience were demanded because faith and obedience were indispensable conditions of assurance in the efficacy of Absolution as dispensed by the Church. A Church which claimed less than the medieval Church would not have been able to make the terrors of medieval religious belief bearable. The extent of the spiritual authority claimed by the medieval Church was a measure of the fears inspired by medieval religious belief.

The essence of the Renaissance consisted, first in the growth of scepticism about the reality of hellfire, and secondly in the consequent growth of scepticism about the spiritual authority of the Church. Post-Reformation Romanism became more and more consciously authoritarian as popular conviction receded about its efficacy against the worst ills that could threaten mankind.

Puritanism emancipated itself from the authority of the medieval Church without emancipating itself from the terrors of medieval religious beliefs. It therefore deprived itself of efficacious spiritual protection without escaping from the necessity for such protection. Puritanism was the individualist substitute for the collective spiritual authority of the medieval Church.

The Church, through its central Sacrifice of the Mass, and through its other ministrations, interpreted the flesh to the Spirit and the Spirit to the flesh and so reconciled the antagonism, inherent in medieval religious belief, between the Spirit and the flesh. For this antagonism was no new thing born of Protestantism and of Puritanism. It is inherent, and always has been inherent, in orthodox Christian belief. Sacramentalism is not merely the technique but the attitude of mind whereby this antagonism is reconciled. In Puritanism there was no such technique, no such attitude of mind.

The anatomy of Puritanism shows the individual human will and the individual human judgment grappling unaided with these problems of reconciliation and absolution. The jaws of hell gaped as widely for the Puritan as they did for the medieval peasant. But, unlike the medieval peasant, he faced them alone. That is the terror of Puritanism. And he faced them unafraid.

That is the glory of Puritanism. To conquer his fear, he built up, with the power of his will, a sombre edifice of energy goaded by diligence, of discipline steeled by repression, of self-confidence buttressed by material success, of certainty informed by Holy Writ and of courage born of the defiant belief that he was, in spite of all, predestined to Salvation in the end.

The Puritan saw life in terms of struggle. For him the object was not reconciliation but victory. *Pilgrim's Progress* is the classic allegory of the Puritan life. And, at the end of the struggle, 'all the trumpets sounded for him on the other side'. That was the crown of and the justification for the struggle.

This concept of struggle explains both the achievements of the outer life of the typical Puritan and the frustrations of his inner life. For the concept of struggle is congruent with a successful approach to the problems of business and administration; it is quite incongruent with a successful approach to the problems of human relationships and of the inner life generally.

The basis of the Puritan's life was the struggle with the evil within himself. His ruthlessness with this internal evil was projected into ruthlessness with external opposition. This too often meant that he was apt to regard as evil, and to pursue with corresponding ruthlessness, that with which he did not happen to agree, and that which happened to be contrary to his material interests.

All good things were derived from God's Grace, but God's Grace only became accessible by the operation of the human will. Therefore, anything pleasant in itself, or any happiness achieved without effort, or apparently bestowed by the human agency of others, tended to be suspect. 'God helps those who help themselves.' That homely Victorian saying conveys much of the very essence of the Puritan religion. God's Grace did not flow; it had to be extracted from the rock. The Puritan God was indeed a jealous God; His favours depended on constant fidelity and on continual prayer.

The value to be put on both material and on spiritual things depended on the amount of will-power and of effort put into them. There was no merit in spontaneity. The way to Heaven was steep and thorny, and it was assumed that any steep and thorny way tended towards Heaven. The path to hell was a primrose path, and it was assumed that any primrose path must tend towards hell.

The first great paradox of Puritanism is the belief in Predestination combined with the immense importance attached to the operation of the human will. The Moslem belief in Fate —which is not dissimilar to the Calvinist belief in Predestination —has precisely the opposite effect in that little importance is attached by devout Moslems to the operation of the human will. But while the Moslem regards himself as the passive instrument of God's Will, the Calvinist regards himself as its active instrument. The Puritan view of the relation between spirit and nature forbade passivity. A belief in Predestination did not dispense with the necessity for the continual exercise of the human will to defeat the promptings of unregenerate nature. Such a belief merely facilitated the process of identifying the Puritan's own will with the Will of God in combating his natural promptings.

In the context of struggle, in which the Puritan saw life, an active instrument of God is necessarily called to unremitting activity. In his internal life he tried to impose what he regarded as the Will of God on his own nature which, by reason of his belief, he regarded as necessarily opposed to the Will of God. The result of this identification of one part of himself—his will—with the Will of God meant that in his external life he did not so much submit himself to God as assume the identification of his whole self and his activities with the Will of God. In the context of his beliefs he assumed, in his external transactions, a conquest which he had not in fact made in his internal life. It does not need modern psychology to enable us to appreciate that the more bitter the internal struggle, the more complete was the assumption of identification with the Will of God in external activities.

The relaxation or the defeat of the human will in its application to the promptings of nature led both to an exaggerated consciousness of sin and to an insidious process of self-justification, by which the unconquered manifestations of unregenerate nature were assimilated to the human will and identified with the Will of God. This consciousness of sin and this self-justification derived on the one hand from the responsibilities involved in and on the other hand from the privileges conferred by Divine Election. Whether or not the Puritan had ceased intellectually and consciously to believe in Divine Election, and whether or not he believed Divine Election to be irrevocable, his habit of mind and of conduct was deeply imbued with a sense of responsibility and a sense of privilege derived from this essential basis of his religious belief. This simultaneous conviction of depravity and of righteousness is the second great paradox of Puritanism. As a result of this paradox, the Puritan was either exaggeratedly ashamed of his weaknesses or else represented them as virtues. He was unable to accept and acknowledge them as ordinary human frailties. This attitude was destructive of ordinary human relationships, since it is difficult to be on terms of intimate friendship with a man who regards himself, in accordance with his prevailing mood, either as a pariah or as a paragon.

The Puritan's life was haunted by the perpetual necessity for satisfying himself that he was elected to Salvation. The evidences of Election were entirely subjective. Whatever inner certainty he might pretend to he was, in the absence of objective tests, in the absence of external authority, necessarily assailed with doubts and necessarily compelled to struggle against these doubts. In this process of struggle, external successes helped to compensate for inner failures and inner successes for external failures. On the one hand, external success was a sign of Divine favour; on the other hand inner righteousness was more important than external success. External success could be seen as deriving from inner righteousness; inner righteousness could be seen as the result of eschewing external success. But, in spite of these possibilities of reassurance, the Puritan soul remained hag-ridden with the fear of hell simultaneously with being exalted by the assurance of Salvation. That is the third great paradox of Puritanism.

The concept of Salvation as a definite state implies the existence of hell as a definite state. Salvation is only conceived as a definite state by one who regards himself as having attained Salvation by an act of Faith. Consciousness of, and consequently fear of, hell only exists in the minds of those who have experienced Salvation. Fear of hell is an inescapable burden incidental to Salvation. The medieval hell, like the medieval heaven, had an objective existence in the minds of the Faithful and, as a result of its supposed objective existence and, so to speak, its communal aspect, lost something of its worst terrors. It was rather like the menace of the hydrogen bomb. Everybody was in the same boat and what was everybody's terror was nobody's terror. But each Puritan had his own lonely hell to which he might be consigned, not as a member of the human race to a collective punishment, but as an individual soul individually cast out by God.

The more the Puritan sought assurance of Salvation in the recognition of special Providences, the more he became convinced of the reality of hell. Involved in such a vicious spiral, something had to break somewhere. It was necessary either to complete the process of liberation begun at the Reformation and to abandon the medieval religious beliefs which Puritanism had inherited, or to take implicit refuge in a modified and respectable Antinomianism by assuming that Election to Salvation automatically and irrevocably removed from the Elect the taint of Original Sin. Ultimately the Puritan was faced with the alternatives of apostacy, hypocrisy or sainthood.

A little scepticism, a little hypocrisy and a little material success all combined to blunt and to pad the bed of nails on which the Puritan was wont to stretch himself. Both the agonies and the ecstasies became less acute with time. But, blunted and padded as they were, the spikes were still there, like the pea in the mattress. Beneath the assured and veneered surfaces of self-satisfaction and success the old fears and doubts, the old meticulousness and the old integrity still lurked, goading with insistent irritations and blighting with subtle poisons. In the flush of health and in the pride of life, Salvation was swallowed up in success and fears of hell relegated to the nursery. But when vitality was low and when the shadows began to fall, the visible world faded and the twin prospects of eternal bliss and eternal fire resumed their supremacy. 'For all that is in the world, the lust of the flesh and the lust of the eyes and the pride of life, is not of the Father, but is of the world. And the world passeth away, and the lust thereof; but he that doeth the Will of God abideth for ever.'

It is easier in this age to imagine the agonies and frustrations rather than the ecstasies and the fulfilments of Puritanism. The Puritan believed that his life was endowed with a special vision and a special purpose which gave an extraordinary significance and dignity to everyday happenings. The vision was derived from his close relationship with God; the purpose was derived from the belief that God was using him as His humble instrument for the working out of His Purposes on earth. If life had the discomforts, the terrors and the possible humiliations of a battlefield, it was also imbued with the excitement, the importance and the interest of a battle. The Puritan belief made everything seem a little larger, a little clearer and a little more immediate. In his own way he had something of the vivid, individual and piercing vision of the artist derived, like the artist's vision, from the belief that he had stripped away certain veils, cleared away certain misunderstandings, in order to apprehend the reality beneath the appearance. Unlike the artist's vision, the Puritan's vision was incommunicable, because the Puritan rejected in advance the only terms in which the apprehension of reality can be made communicable. Just as the artist might see significant form in the flight of a kingfisher, so the Puritan might see a special Providence in the fall of a sparrow. To the Puritan the recognition of special Providences in everyday things was like the artist's recognition of beauty in everyday things. For that reason the Puritan, like the artist, could afford to dispense with entertainment. This sense of the significance of everyday things helps to explain the typical Puritan contempt for art which, at best, he held to be but a reflected vision of that which he claimed to be able to apprehend directly.

But more important than this heightened sense of vision was that conviction of being carried along in the current of God's Purpose, a conviction which no sense of sin, no consciousness of unworthiness, no setbacks, no hardships and no failures could altogether obliterate. He was 'on the Lord's side' and, though he might sin like David and suffer undeserved misfortunes like Job, it was all part of God's inscrutable Purpose, and all would come right in the end.

This belief is congruent with, and obviously derived from, the similar belief expressed time and again in the Psalms and in the Old Testament generally. Continual Bible reading created, and subsequently nourished, Puritan beliefs. In the Psalms one finds the best expression, and perhaps the best explanation, both of Puritan agonies and of Puritan ecstasies. And how many times were Puritan cruelties justified by the story of David and the Amalekites; how many times were Puritan frailties compared with, and comfort taken as a result from, David's behaviour over Bathsheba and Uriah the Hittite? How many times were disobedient children compared with Absalom; how many times were tiresome opponents compared with Saul? And how many times, perhaps, was David's love for Jonathan used to justify unnatural concupiscence?

But Salvation was only compatible with sinfulness because of Christ's Sacrifice in taking the sins of mankind upon Himself. The sins of the Elect did not, in the Puritan's more optimistic moments, imperil Salvation, but they did both add to the burden of sin borne by Christ and add to the weight of obligation owed to Christ for His work of Redemption. It is impossible here to discuss Puritan Christology, but it may be suggested that perhaps the most specifically Christian aspect of Puritanism was an acute sensitiveness to the enormity of sin, as being both a failure to follow Christ's Divine Example, and as being an additional burden of sorrow laid upon the Redeemer of mankind. In spite of the extent to which the Old Testament was used for purposes of self-justification, there was always the consciousness that, because of Christ's Example and of Christ's Sacrifice, a higher standard of conduct was expected by God from man after the Incarnation than before. Failure to observe this higher standard not only led to agonies of remorse, but also to the birth of doubts about the irrevocability of Salvation. Thus the sense of ecstasy derived from a special vision of God, and from a special identification with God's Purpose, was inextricably mixed with a fear of expulsion from the Divine Presence and of separation from the Divine Purpose.

The heights, as well as the depths, of Puritan experience were flattened out in process of time. But just as the depths were momentarily re-experienced in times of lowered vitality, so were the heights momentarily re-experienced in times of keenness and crisis. Even in the nineteenth century, when Salvation had been secularized into respectability and when disreputability had become the earthly equivalent of damnation, angels as well as devils occasionally visited the Puritan soul in its self-imposed loneliness. But, apart from these occasional visitations, in the counting-house or in the factory, in the council chamber or in the bosom of his family, the respectable Puritan was still instinctively conscious of the distant beating of angels' wings and the distant smoke from an everlasting fire. Even though considerations of earthly prudence had largely replaced both the hope of heaven and the fear of hell as the principal arbiter of conduct, his lips still repeated and his mind still half-believed doctrines which served as a link between the street of a Victorian suburb and the field of a Cromwellian victory.

Puritanism was not wholly an English social and religious phenomenon. Calvinist Protestantism produced similar characteristics in Switzerland, in Scandinavia and in Scotland. Puritanism in its most extreme and rigid form developed in the New England colonies of North America, peopled by the descendants of refugees from religious persecution in England. The Norwegian provincial society depicted in Ibsen's plays describes a Puritan society at the height of its economic power and at the beginning of its spiritual decline, which would be applicable in most of its details to English or to New England middle-class society at the same time. It is noticeable that in all cases the specific characteristics of Puritanism declined as the hold of Calvinism weakened. It seems reasonable to assume that Calvinist Protestantism, rather than any matter of race or economics, was the common origin of the phenomenon of Puritanism.

On this assumption Puritanism can be regarded either as a

stage in the liberation of society from the fetters of Christianity, or as a perversion of Christianity, or as a development towards a perfect form of Christianity, or as the particular form of Christianity ordained by Christ.

From the Puritan point of view, and this is what distinguishes Puritanism from other forms of Protestantism, pure Christianity was conceived of, not as a process of development, but as a reversion to apostolic Christianity. In spite of Robinson's famous remark about there being more light yet to come out of God's Word, orthodox Puritanism never admitted the possibility of any development in Christianity, which was conceived as existing whole, entire and perfect in the Church of the Apostles, without the possibility of any future discovery being made, either by reason or by revelation.

The Catholic conception of the Church as being a universal, authoritative and continuing source of Divine Revelation provides a convention by which the Christian Faith can become enriched with experience without losing its cohesion. The lack of any such authority in Puritanism resulted in a continual struggle with obscurantism and incoherence, combined with a dangerous and ever-widening gap between the assumptions of orthodox religious belief and the assumptions of everyday scientific knowledge. This gap was unbridgeable because the Puritan rejected in advance any kind of intermediary, in the form of organization, Sacrament, or Image, between himself and God. He rejected as a barrier that which, to the Catholic, was a means of communication. The result was that the gap could not be bridged; it could only be jumped. The basic assumption of antagonism between nature and spirit was paralleled by the antagonism which grew up between science and religion. A Puritan could only accept the assumptions of science by abandoning the doctrines of his religion; he could only accept the doctrines of his religion by abandoning the assumptions of science. He could jump from one to the other; he could not achieve any sort of synthesis between the two. The recent history of the Nonconformist Churches illustrates the attempts made to achieve such a synthesis, and seems to illustrate the view that such a synthesis can only be found in an abandonment of the basic assumptions of Puritanism.

Accepting the Christian basis of Puritanism, where does Puritanism stand in its relation to Christianity? From the beginning there can be observed a dualism in Puritan belief which on the one hand identified it with secular forces of progress and development, and on the other hand caused it to reject any possibility of progress or development in the Christian religion. As time went on this dualism caused increasing tensions. Puritanism was like a piece of elastic joining two pieces of wood being drawn in contrary directions. The tension became greater and greater until the elastic either snapped or lost its elasticity.

From this point of view, Puritanism can be regarded either as a stage towards the abandonment of Christianity altogether—a retreat to the Apostles as to a last ditch—or as a heresy—a wrong turning in the path of the Christian Faith. For it cannot seriously be contended that an ever-increasing state of tension between two sides of a man's existence can represent the particular form of Christianity ordained by Christ, and the very nature of Puritanism precludes it from being regarded as a development towards a form of Christianity not already attained by the Apostles.

These two alternatives are really one, since the valid objection to heresy is not that it represents a divergence from the orthodox 'line', but that it represents a divergence from the thing itself, which will ultimately lead to the abandonment of the thing itself. Historically, in its relation to the Christian Faith, Puritanism bears out this point of view. Ultimately, the Puritan has only remained a Christian to the extent of his abandonment of Puritanism. The Puritan tendency to Unitarianism and to 'Freethought' in the eighteenth century, and to scientific humanism and the 'social gospel' in the nineteenth were not relapses from, but logical developments of, Puritan Christianity.

The heresy of Puritanism, like most other heresies, was due, not to any false belief, but to the exaggeration of some, and to the denial of other, aspects of true belief. The individual aspect of Christianity was exaggerated at the expense of the corporate aspect; the difference between nature and spirit was exaggerated into an antagonism between them; the omnipotence of God was exaggerated into a denial of freewill; distrust of idolatry was exaggerated into a repudiation of every kind of imagery. These exaggerations and these denials were reflected in the Puritan character and in Puritan actions.

The effect therefore of Puritanism was one not of falsity but of distortion. The individual virtues were magnified, the social virtues atrophied; the qualities of energy and of will-power were developed at the expense of the qualities of understanding and of harmony. The design of Puritanism remained coherent and rigid so long as the human resources of will and energy which maintained it remained sufficiently powerful to withstand the tremendous and increasing human and social tensions set up within the design. The continuing power of these resources was maintained both by the religious faith which generated it and by the material success which seemed to justify it. When these failed the design collapsed into ruins.

The original and simultaneous impulse towards Puritanism over so much of Western Europe seems to have been an aspect of that general intellectual impulse to seek inspiration and renewal from the past which characterized the movement of Renaissance. Culturally, Western Europe at the end of the fifteenth century was in a verisimilar position to the Roman Empire at the dawn of the Christian era. Old ideas and old institutions were seen as inadequate in the light of new horizons. The newly discovered access to ancient learning and to ancient methods of thought fired men with the idea that the secret of the future lay in the correct interpretation of the past. Apostolic religion was of a piece with classical architecture, in its simplicity, in the purity of its outline and in the uncritical attitude towards it adopted by its devotees.

Puritanism was the specific reaction of certain classes in certain conditions to new ideas and new opportunities. The classical propensities of the movement of Renaissance dictated that this reaction should seek inspiration from the memorials of antiquity. For the Puritans the Apostles were the Christian equivalent of the classics.

The religious atmosphere in Northern Europe dictated that the reaction should have a religious basis and also dictated that the reaction should be grounded in the religious prejudices of the time. The classes who embraced Puritanism felt the need for release from certain servitudes which were identified in their minds with certain political and ecclesiastical institutions. They did not feel the need for intellectual freedom and did not therefore seek release from the intellectual servitudes implied by certain of their religious beliefs. This background caused them to regard the ecclesiastical apparatus of Romanism and, to a lesser extent, the ecclesiastical apparatus of Anglicanism as being, not an interpretation of, but a barrier against their religious beliefs. In their preoccupation with the political and social implications of this ecclesiastical apparatus, they rejected its spiritual significance. But because they retained the beliefs which gave to this ecclesiastical apparatus its spiritual justification, they imposed upon themselves the necessity for dealing individually with the problems created by these religious beliefs. This necessity on the one hand developed some of the qualities required for material advancement and on the other hand set up irreconcilable antagonisms in respect of those ambitions and desires which are inseparable from and nourished by material advancement. The spiritual burden of trying to interpret medieval Christianity without accepting the convention of ecclesiastical authority both provided the power which sustained, and imposed the limitations which circumscribed, the course of English Puritanism. The relinquishment of that burden marks the end of English Puritanism. But the qualities and defects evolved in the course of that burden's carriage survive and form part of the English tradition.

Bibliography

THIS 'Bibliography' is simply a record of those books bearing on the subject which I happened to read while preparing to write, and while actually writing, this book. It has no claim to being a comprehensive list of books on the subject of English Puritanism.

The Influence of Puritanism in the Political and Religious Thought of England. J. S. Flynn. Murray. 1920.

The Holy Spirit in Puritan Faith and Experience. G. F. Nuttall. Blackwell. 1946.

National Character and the Factors in its Formation. Sir Ernest Barker. Methuen. 1948. (4th ed.)

Medieval Panorama. G. G. Coulton. Cambridge. 1947 ed.

The Merchant Class of Medieval London. Sylvia Thrupp. Chicago Univ. 1948.

The Reign of Elizabeth. J. B. Black. Oxford. 1936.

England Under the Stuarts. G. M. Trevelyan. 1904. (11th ed. Methuen. 1924.)

Oliver Cromwell. John Buchan. Hodder & Stoughton. 1934.

Social Studies in Carolean England. David Mathew. Oxford. 1948.

King Charles and King Pym, 1637–1643. E. W. Stratford. Hollis and Carter. 1949.

Henry VIII and the Reformation. H. Maynard Smith. Macmillan. 1948.

The Puritans in England. W. H. Stowell. Nelson. 1849.

The Church in England. S. C. Carpenter. Murray. 1954.

English Puritanism and Its Leaders. Tulloch. Blackwood. 1861.

The History of the Puritans. Daniel Neal. (4 vols.) Baynes. 1822.

Puritan Manifestoes. W. H. Frere & C. E. Douglas. S.P.C.K. 1907.

The Laws of Ecclesiastical Polity. Richard Hooker. (3 vols.) Oxford ed. 1888.

Religion and the Rise of Capitalism. R. H. Tawney. Murray. 1929.

The Story of Quakerism (1652–1952). Elfrida Vipont. Bennisdale Press. 1954.

Wesley and His Century. Rev. W. H. Fitchett. Smith, Elder. 1906.

Wesley's Legacy to the World. J. Ernest Rattenbury. Epworth Press. 1928.

Wilberforce. Sir Reginald Coupland. Collins. 1945.

Histoire de Peuple Anglais au 19me. Siècle. Elie Halevy. (4 vols.) Hachette. 1923.

The Evangelical Revival in the Eighteenth Century. Rev. J. H. Overton. Longmans, Green. 1886.

The Unitarian Contribution to Social Progress. Raymond V. Holt. Lindsey Press. 1952.

A History of the English Baptists. A. C. Underwood. Kingsgate Press. 1947.

History of English Congregationalism. R. W. Dale. Hodder & Stoughton. 1907.

A Serious Call to a Devout and Holy Life. William Law. Everyman ed.

The English Church in the Nineteenth Century (1800–1833). J. H. Overton. Longmans, Green. 1894.

Freedom and Organization, 1814–1914. Bertrand Russell. Allen & Unwin. 1934.

The Growth of English Society. E. Lipson. A. & C. Black. 1949.

Wesley's England. J. S. Whately. Epworth Press. 1938.

A History of the English People, 1895–1905. Elie Halevy. (tr. E. I. Watkin.) Benn. 1929.

The Bleak Age. J. L. & Barbara Hammond. Pelican ed. 1947.

Lord Shaftesbury. J. L. & Barbara Hammond. Pelican ed. 1939.

The Acquisitive Society. R. H. Tawney. Bell. 1930.

Milton in the Puritan Revolution. Don M. Wolfe. Nelson. 1941.

Victorian Period Piece. J. S. Leatherbarrow. S.P.C.K. 1943.

Autobiography. J. S. Mill. Longmans, Green. 1873.

Jeremy Bentham. C. M. Atkinson. Methuen. 1925.

Gordon. H. E. Wortham. Harrap. 1933.

Gladstone. Philip Magnus. Murray. 1954.

Free Churchmanship in England, 1870–1940. John W. Grant. Independent Press. 1955.

Reason and Revolution. Herbert Marcuse. Routledge and Kegan Paul. 1955.

Tudor Puritanism. M. M. Knappen. Chicago Univ. 1939.

English Puritanism, 1660–88. C. E. Whiting. S.P.C.K. 1931.

The Puritans. Perry Miller & Thos. H. Johnson. American Book Co. 1938.

The Protestant Tradition. J. S. Whale. Cambridge. 1955.

INDEX

Date Due

OCT 31 '63			
pd APR 9 '64			